LIFE'S
TOOLBOX
tools for coping with life

Rick Carter, Jr., Ph.D.

LIFE'S
TOOLBOX
tools for coping with life

Rick Carter, Jr., Ph.D.

ISBN# 978-1-61119-026-7

Printed in the United States of America.

Printed by Calvary Publishing
A Ministry of Parker Memorial Baptist Church
1902 East Cavanaugh Road
Lansing, Michigan 48910
www.CalvaryPublishing.org

Calvary PUBLISHING
FOR BAPTISTS BY BAPTISTS
CP KJV
A ministry of Parker Memorial Baptist Church
1902 East Cavanaugh Road • Lansing, Michigan 48910
Phone: 517.882.2112 • Fax: 517.882.2317
www.calvarypublishing.org

Contents

Acknowledgments

The Lord has been gracious to teach me through so many ways and so many people the glorious truths of His Word. This book is a collection of those lessons that I have learned.

I want to give a special thanks to my wife Angela, for her faithfulness and submissive spirit in following the work of the Lord in our lives.

Thank you to my Father Rick Carter Sr. for the love, prayer, and teaching that He instilled in my life.

Thank you to my teacher Dr. Mike Hays, for his faithfulness to the Lord and His Word. Many of these things were learned through the ministry of the Biblical Counselors Seminary and the teaching of Dr. Hays.

Thank you to my pastor Dr. Ivan Casteel, for his godly example and patient teaching in my life as well.

Last but not least, thank you to the congregation of the Beth Haven Baptist Church, of Oklahoma City, Oklahoma. It is my great blessing to be your pastor and have the opportunity to work on these and many other projects as a result of your faithfulness and love.

CHAPTER ONE

Overcoming Traumatic Events

According to the national center for post-traumatic stress disorder web site, 60.7% of men and 51.2% of women report at least one traumatic event in their life. We live in a world that is wrecked with the effects of sin. Just being a Christian is not a free pass from the consequences that sin has brought into our world. Jesus reminded us in Matthew 5:45 **"That ye may be the children of your Father which is in heaven: for he maketh his sun to rise on the evil and on the good, and sendeth rain on the just and on the unjust."** In my own life, I have had several traumatic events, from an auto accident, to standing over my daughter in the emergency room not knowing what was wrong. Some traumatic events pass quickly, while some, however, have devastating lingering effects. Maybe you are reading this book and you have experienced something much more devastating than I. I have counseled with people who have been molested, and with those who have lost loved ones in unfortunate ways. I have found that the Bible answer works no matter what the cause of trauma in life. So how are we to respond when we face a traumatic event in life? The Bible gives us a great insight into what we need to do through David. Psalm 109 was a passage written as David was in flight from Saul. Three separate attempts were made on David's life while he was in Saul's palace, then he was hunted like an animal. David was a man who certainly knew about traumatic events in life. His message to us in Psalms gives us a great wealth of help.

There are five prominent things in this passage that we will look at. The first section is in verses 1-5, **"Hold not thy peace, O God of my praise; For the mouth of the wicked and the mouth of the deceitful are opened against me: they have spoken against me with a lying tongue. They compassed me about also with words of hatred; and fought against me without a cause. For my love they are my adversaries: but I** *give myself unto* **prayer. And they have rewarded me evil for good, and hatred for my love."** In this passage we find out three things the victim of trauma feels.

1. We see first that David feels that the peace of God has been withheld from him. Have you felt the same way, that there is no peace in your life since your traumatic event? John 14:27 **"Peace I leave with you, my peace I give unto you: not as the**

world giveth, give I unto you. Let not your heart be troubled, neither let it be afraid." God desires you to have peace beyond human understanding. He says so in Philippians 4:7 "**And the peace of God, which passeth all understanding, shall keep your hearts and minds through Christ Jesus.**" It is not God that has taken your peace; it is only when we let the Devil distort the truth that we lose peace. As we come to the end of this chapter, we are going to see two things that will restore peace.

2. The next thing that David felt was that others were talking about what had happened to him. The feeling of paranoia, that everyone else is watching and talking about you, is expressed several times in this chapter. David did not always succumb to these feelings, and as a matter of fact, in Psalm 56:8-11 "**Thou tellest my wanderings: put thou my tears into thy bottle: *are they* not in thy book? When I *cry unto* thee, then shall mine enemies turn back: this I know; for God *is* for me. In God will I praise *his* word: in the LORD will I praise *his* word. In God have I put my trust: I will not be afraid what man can do unto me.**" This passage shows us not only that God is actively involved in every tear that you cry, but is also ready to deliver you from all your enemies. There is no need to fear man when God is for you.

3. The third feeling that David had was that he

was innocent of any wrong doing and that he received hatred for his love. Many times in cases of violence and sexual offences, it is done by someone known to you. The travesty of molestation has increased dramatically in our society, and is most often committed by a family member. Many times the victims blame themselves and it affects the rest of their lives. It can cause marital trouble because of fear of intimacy or lack of trust. The victims very often become bitter, and not always at the offender. Sometimes it is at those they thought should have protected them, and even sometimes at themselves.

The next section of verses are called imprecatory, which means that the author is telling God what he wishes would happen to the offender. Verses 6-20 say, **"Set thou a wicked man over him: and let Satan stand at his right hand. When he shall be judged, let him be condemned: and let his prayer become sin. Let his days be few;** *and* **let another take his office. Let his children be fatherless, and his wife a widow. Let his children be continually vagabonds, and beg: let them seek** *their bread* **also out of their desolate places. Let the extortioner catch all that he hath; and let the strangers spoil his labour. Let there be none to extend mercy unto him: neither let there be any to favour his fatherless children. Let his posterity be cut off;** *and* **in the generation following**

let their name be blotted out. Let the iniquity of his fathers be remembered with the LORD; and let not the sin of his mother be blotted out. Let them be before the LORD continually, that he may cut off the memory of them from the earth. Because that he remembered not to shew mercy, but persecuted the poor and needy man, that he might even slay the broken in heart. As he loved cursing, so let it come unto him: as he delighted not in blessing, so let it be far from him. As he clothed himself with cursing like as with his garment, so let it come into his bowels like water, and like oil into his bones. Let it be unto him as the garment _which_ covereth him, and for a girdle wherewith he is girded continually. _Let_ this _be_ the reward of mine adversaries from the LORD, and of them that speak evil against my soul."

Now you may be inclined to reprimand David for expressing those things, but if you are honest with yourself, you have felt the same way. The Devil has a way of using those things to accuse you. He may have said to you that a Christian wouldn't feel that way. You may have even convinced yourself that it was sin to even have those feelings. Let's take a reality check. David was a man after God's own heart; there was no one closer to God. Reading the Psalms, you see a man who was very yielded to God, and even David had those feelings. He even wrote a song about them. He told God about how he felt. Did you know that it is OK to tell God how you feel? He knows anyway, so you are not hiding it from Him. God created you with feelings. It is not OK to react to life based on your feelings, but you are going to have feelings. The wonderful thing about feelings is that they can be changed. David begins that change in the next verse as he declares what he wants God to do for him.

Verse 21 says, **"But do thou for me, O GOD the Lord, for thy name's sake: because thy mercy *is* good, deliver thou me."** David wanted what everyone who has experienced traumatic events in life wants: mercy and deliverance. David has been honest with God. In the same way, it is important to bear your heart to God. Psalm 51:6 **"Behold, thou desirest truth in the inward parts: and in the hidden *part* thou shalt make me to know wisdom."** God will not save someone until they confess their sin in repentance. Understand that David was not coming to force God to do his own will; he was simply confessing to God that he has had these feelings toward someone else. Then saying in effect, *"But God, I don't want these feelings, what I really want is mercy and deliverance. I want to be delivered from the pain that is in my heart right now. I want you to show mercy on me and give me peace instead of hurt."* Be careful that you do your confessing to God and not to other people. It can become sin if you let it become gossip. God is not glorified in the bad feelings themselves, He is glorified in the fact that you bring them to Him recognizing that He is the only one that can deliver you from them.

Verses 22-25 examine four of the emotional consequences that accompany trauma. **"For I *am* poor and needy, and my heart is wounded within me. I am gone like the shadow when it declineth: I am tossed up and down as the locust. My knees are weak through fasting; and my flesh faileth of fatness. I became also a reproach unto them: *when* they looked upon me they shaked their heads."**

1. You may have a wounded heart. You may feel a deep hurt that you are unsure whether you can ever recover from. You may have fallen prey to the feeling that you can never feel "normal" again. Beware of the extreme thinking of "never" and "always." Few things in life are this way, and by following the Scriptures you can overcome this trial, too. Remember Philippians 4:13 **"I can do all things through Christ which strengtheneth me."**

2. The second emotional consequence is that of withdrawing. The Psalmist says that he is gone like the shadow when it declineth. Have you withdrawn from others? Do you desire to be alone instead of facing people? Have you had an emotional withdraw, building up walls so that people cannot get

close enough to hurt you? You may have thought something was wrong with you, when the truth is that you are responding just as a normal person does, just like David did. Hold on! God has an answer coming for you; He has deliverance for you.

3. Next, the Psalmist says that he is tossed up and down like the locust. We may express this by saying, *"I'm on an emotional roller coaster. I can't seem to control my emotions."* Remember this was the same response King David had before he applied the cure that God gave him.

4. The last emotional consequence David experienced was that he had a sudden health change. He lost weight, a noticeable altering of his physical appearance. Those around him could see the change. You may have experienced the opposite, gaining weight instead of losing it. You may have become trapped in a cycle of eating disorders. If you have fallen into an eating disorder since your traumatic event, you need to be cautious that you are not giving heed to doctrines of Devils as it says in I Timothy 4:1-3.

So what is the answer? How did David go on and overcome this traumatic event? More specifically, how can you overcome the trauma that you have experienced? The answer is two parts and is found in the last few verses of the chapter. Verses 26-30, **"Help me, O LORD my God: O save me accord-**

ing to thy mercy: That they may know that this *is* thy hand; *that* thou, LORD, hast done it. Let them curse, but bless thou: when they arise, let them be ashamed; but let thy servant rejoice. Let mine adversaries be clothed with shame, and let them cover themselves with their own confusion, as with a mantle. I will greatly praise the LORD with my mouth; yea, I will praise him among the multitude."

The first step that David took was to acknowledge that everything that happened to him, happened by the will of God. Wait a minute! I didn't say God did it. What I did say is that the Scripture teaches us that God prohibits or allows ALL things that happen to us in life. The Biblical example of this is Job. In Job 1:6-12 it says, **"Now there was a day when the sons of God came to present themselves before the LORD, and Satan came also among them. And the LORD said unto Satan, Whence, comest thou? Then Satan answered the LORD, and said, From going to and fro in the earth, and from walking up and down in it. And the LORD said unto Satan, Hast thou considered my servant Job, that *there is* none like him in the earth, a perfect and an upright man, one that feareth God, and escheweth evil? Then Satan answered the LORD, and said, Doth Job fear God for nought? Hast not thou made an hedge about**

him, and about his house, and about all that he hath on every side? thou hast blessed the work of his hands, and his substance is increased in the land. But put forth thine hand now, and touch all that he hath, and he will curse thee to thy face. And the LORD said unto Satan, Behold, all that he hath *is* **in thy power; only upon himself put not forth thine hand. So Satan went forth from the presence of the LORD.**" Here we find that Satan was not able to attack Job due to the hedge of thorns that God had placed around him and all that he had. Even when God allowed Satan access to Job, he was still limited in what he could do.

You may ask the same question that many have: Why would God allow the Devil access to me? Job's friends had all sorts of reasons why, and none of them were right. The conclusion of Job seems to be that God is God, and He does not have to answer to you nor me. We look at life in a finite manner; we do not see the whole picture. God sees not only where we are now, but also where we are going. He knows that there are things we will never learn without trauma. I had a friend die at a young age several years ago. I began to ask the question, why did You have to take someone so young? Then God directed me to I Kings 14:12-13 **"Arise thou therefore, get thee to thine own house:** *and* **when thy feet enter into the city, the child shall die. And all Israel**

shall mourn for him, and bury him: for he only of Jeroboam shall come to the grave, because in him there is found *some* **good thing toward the LORD God of Israel in the house of Jeroboam."** God was preparing to judge the house of Jeroboam. This child of Jeroboam was taken to keep him from the judgment that was going to befall his father's house. God was being merciful to him. God's mercy is sometimes seen by us as a catastrophe. Job found a truth in chapter 19:6 **"Know now that God hath overthrown me, and hath compassed me with his net."** It is God that allowed the trauma in Job's life.

Acknowledging this takes power away from your enemy. Those who have traumatized you have no power over you if you acknowledge that God is in control of all things that happen in your life. You may remember Romans 8:28 which says, **"And we know that all things work together for good to them that love God, to them who are the called according to** *his* **purpose."** The Scripture does not tell us that all things that happen to those who love God will be good. Many things that happen are bad. God did not promise to keep all bad things from happening to us, but He did promise that if we will allow Him to work His will in our lives, that all things good and bad would work together for good. I believe that the two verses prior to this verse give us an indication of the fact that bad things happen in life when they say, **"Likewise the Spirit also helpeth our infirmities: for we know not what we should pray for as we ought: but the Spirit itself maketh intercession for us with groanings which cannot be uttered. And he that searcheth the hearts knoweth what *is* the mind of the Spirit, because he maketh intercession for the saints according to *the will of* God."** God is saying that when you cannot understand why things have happened in your life, when you do not even know how to pray, He knows what you need.

Traumatic events bring us to an end of our abilities. They bring us to the place that we have to turn to God, when there are no other options. It is at those times that God says, turn to me and I will make these bad things in life work together for good. Your enemy has power over you as long as you believe that they control what they did to you. When you change that belief and acknowledge that they could do nothing to you except what God allowed, then they are powerless. No longer do you need to fear them. No longer do they have the power; now all things are as they should be. All power belongs to God. He is in control and we are yielded to His authority.

The next thing that David did was to praise God for what had happened to him. 1 Thessalonians 5:18

"In every thing give thanks: for this is the will of God in Christ Jesus concerning you." It is not just God's will for you to give thanks when things get worked out for good, but to give thanks for the traumatic events that happen to you as well. This is a very difficult thing to do, to actually thank God for the bad thing that happened to you. This is a foreign concept to us, but is exactly what the Scripture requires for us to do. Ephesians 5:20 **"Giving thanks always for all things unto God and the Father in the name of our Lord Jesus Christ;"**

Praising God for the traumatic event that happened in your life takes power away from the adversary, the Devil. Do you remember what the Devil said Job would do if God removed the hedge of protection from him? He said that Job would curse God to his face. What do you suppose it does to the Devil, when instead of causing you to curse God, you begin to praise God for the trauma in life? The last thing that the Devil wants is to see God praised. Praising God for trauma is a sure way to get the Devil to flee.

Praising God also begins to remove the cloud of depression that often shrouds those who have been burdened down with trauma. Isaiah 61:3 **"To appoint unto them that mourn in Zion, to give unto them beauty for ashes, the oil of joy for mourning, the garment of praise for the spirit of heavi-**

ness; that they might be called trees of righteousness, the planting of the LORD, that he might be
glorified." Praising God takes your mind off of you
and puts it on Him. It also trains your mind to think
on things that are profitable to you. Philippians 4:8
says, **"Finally, brethren, whatsoever things are
true, whatsoever things *are* honest, whatsoever
things *are* just, whatsoever things *are* pure, whatsoever things *are* lovely, whatsoever things *are* of
good report; if *there be* any virtue, and if *there be*
any praise, think on these things."** Praising God is
the essence of thinking on these things. It may help
you to make lists of things that you are thankful to
God for. You can use a notebook or 3x5 cards. Make
it a habit to list more things every day. Daniel did
this three times each day. Daniel 6:10 **"Now when
Daniel knew that the writing was signed, he went
into his house; and his windows being open in
his chamber toward Jerusalem, he kneeled upon
his knees three times a day, and prayed, and gave
thanks before his God, as he did aforetime."**

David praised God seven times a day. Psalm
119:164 **"Seven times a day do I praise thee because of thy righteous judgments."** You would be
surprised how many things that you have to thank
God for. You should thank Him for everything you
can see. If you have an enemy, you should look for
things about them to thank God for. Even in the

worst circumstances we are to thank God.

Once you have done these two things, acknowledging God's control in your life and praising Him for the trauma in your life, then you will have given all the power back to God. That is when He will take all things and work them together to good. David ended Psalm 109 with verse 31, **"For he shall stand at the right hand of the poor, to save *him* from those that condemn his soul."** You see, God stands ready to deliver and save you from condemnation. It may be from the condemnation of others, or it may be from yourself. When you give to God the position and praise He is due, it opens the door to Him to deliver you.

CHAPTER TWO

I'm Offended

Matthew 18:7, **"Woe unto the world because of offences! for it must needs be that offences come; but woe to that man by whom the offence cometh!"** Jesus speaking here has given us a key truth in being able to deal properly with offences. This truth is that offences against us are inevitable. There is no such place as a place of no offences. God allows offences to come into your life to test you and to help you grow; the key is how we respond to offence in our lives. There is a difference in being offended (what others do to us), and taking offence (what we do to ourselves). The difference between the two is how we respond to it. The Biblical response to someone offending us is to forgive them. Matthew 18:21-22 says, **"Then came Peter to him, and said, Lord, how oft shall my brother sin against me, and I forgive him? till seven times? Jesus saith unto him, I say not unto thee, Until seven times: but, Until seventy times seven."** Peter thought that forgiving someone for offending him seven times was a great feat of Christian growth, but Jesus told him to forgive seventy times more than his best guess. The term seventy times seven was meant to imply an infinite number of times. Jesus was in effect saying to Peter, be offended and forgive, but do not ever take offence. To take offence means that we put on the air of being offended. When we take offence we want everyone to know we are not happy with them. It is not Biblical to act in this manner. Allow me to use an illustration: when a child gets offended at their parents and doesn't know how to deal with it properly they will throw themselves down on the floor, kick and scream, cry and whine, we call this a temper tantrum. When an adult takes offence they act much the same way, only in a more socially acceptable manner. The heart of the matter is the same, they puff up like a horny toad to let everyone around them know that they are unhappy. The truth of the matter is that Biblically happiness is your choice.

If you are frequently offended, I want you to know that this chapter is written in love and with a sincere desire to help you overcome the traps of Satan. This chapter is not to coddle you; it is written to help you overcome. It is not God's plan for a person to be constantly taking offense. We must come to one realization right off the bat, that taking offence is something you have done, not something that was done to you. Many times we can get into the rut of believing that our being offended is other people's fault, but it isn't. Now I am not saying that others never do anything wrong, or never do bad to you; I am saying that taking offence at what others do is entirely up to you. You are in control of your own spirit and your own will, and a person that takes offence at everything others do will be a person who is perpetually unhappy, and will run off those around them.

In this chapter we will be looking at the Biblical causes for people being offended, the consequences of being offended for the offended person, and the cure for being offended.

There are four Biblical causes for a person taking offence. The first cause is the source of most all of our troubles: it is that old word pride. Proverbs 13:10 **"Only by pride cometh contention: but with the well advised *is* wisdom."** Many times we are so filled up with pride that anything that we perceive as a slight to ourselves we immediately take offence to. Pride is a self exalting feeling that you either think you are better, or that you deserve to be treated better. Pride is called in the Bible the great transgression, and it is the sin that turned the angel Lucifer into the Devil. He was lifted up in pride and took offence that God did not exalt him above everything. His action of taking offence made him the enemy of God. Taking offense makes you act like the Devil and it separates you from God as well, you may think that you have righteous anger, but it is really self-righteous anger and is against God.

Another reason people take offense is because they are trying to divert focus away from themselves. In John chapter 8, the Pharisees brought a woman to Jesus that they were offended at for the fact that she had committed adultery. Jesus said to them in verse seven, **"…He that is without sin among you, let him first cast a stone at her."** He then stooped down and wrote in the dirt, the Bible gives their response in verse 9, **"And they which heard *it*, being convicted by *their own* conscience, went out one by one, beginning at the eldest, *even* unto the last: and Jesus was left alone, and the woman standing in the midst."** You see, their conviction was confronted by Jesus and they forgot about the offense of the woman. I have seen many people under conviction of God to deal with something in their life that they didn't want to deal with. Many times I have seen them take up some offense in order to divert the attention off of themselves and use it as an excuse not to get right with God. Many times the offense they take up belongs to someone else. It is like they become crusaders for anyone who they perceive as being offended. Proverbs 26:17 says, **"He that passeth by, *and* meddleth with strife be-**

longing **not to him,** *is like* **one that taketh a dog by the ears."** Taking on an offense that is not yours is like grabbing a dog by the ears: you are the one that is going to get bitten. It is far better to simply deal with your conviction than to look for offenses to mask it.

A third reason people take offense according the Bible is that the offended person lacks sufficient Christian character. Matthew 13:21 says, **"Yet hath he not root in himself, but dureth for a while: for when tribulation or persecution ariseth because of the word, by and by he is offended."** The phrase hath not root in himself means that his character is not deep. He is easily offended because he has not yet grown and matured in Christ, digging out the rocks and stumps in his life so that he can be a fruitful field for God. Everyone of us has things in our lives that are stumbling stones. As people come through our life, if we don't remove these stumbling stones, others will stumble over these areas, and they or we will become offended when this happens. An immature person takes offense at little things; a person who grows up into maturity is less likely to be offended. I have heard people say to each other things like, "grow up", "just be an adult", "don't be so juvenile", or "how junior high." The issue is not just being emotionally immature, it is being spiritually immature, as well. Even an emotionally mature lost man will not be able to handle many offenses, but a spiritually mature man will be able to control his spirit and forgive. God gives an example of each of these in proverbs. Proverbs 25:28 says, **"He that hath no rule over his own spirit *is like* a city *that is* broken down, *and* without walls."** Proverbs 16:32 says, **"*He that is* slow to anger *is* better than the mighty; and he that ruleth his spirit than he that taketh a city."**

The last reason given in the Bible is that they lack love for God and His Word. Psalm 119:165 says, **"Great peace have they which love thy law: and nothing shall offend them."** A sincere love for God and His Word will cause us to forgive our brothers when they trespass against us, overlooking their faults that would otherwise offend us. 1 Peter 4:8 says, **"And above all things have fervent charity among yourselves: for charity shall cover the multitude of sins."** When we take offense, we are telling on our love for God and His Word. When I find myself taking offense at what others have done, the first thing I do is examine my walk with God. Even someone who is grounded in the Lord can struggle with this when they are not walking with the Lord as they should. When we are not faithful in the Word our love slacks off from what it should be. Little things become grievous to us and we begin to act in the flesh if we are not walking in a fervent relationship with God. Being filled with the Spirit is the ultimate weapon against this issue.

If you are someone who takes offense, you need to know that there are serious consequences listed in the Bible for doing so. One of the things people will eventually do if they take offense is to turn away from following after Jesus. Did you realize that many people were offended at Jesus? What does this tell you? Does it say to you that Jesus was offensive or that they were not following God? Matthew 13:57 says, **"And they were offended in him. But Jesus said unto them, A prophet is not without honour, save in his own country, and in his own house."** In John, Jesus was preaching and many people got offended by His message. It says in John 6:66-67, **"From that *time* many of his disciples went back, and walked no more with him. Then said Jesus unto the twelve, Will ye also go away?"** If you notice, Jesus did not run after them and say He was sorry that He offended them. Telling them the truth was not the problem, the problem was that they didn't love His law, nor did they love Him enough to follow Him when it went against their feelings. Many people have been offended and used it as an excuse to stop following Jesus Christ. We must be like Peter in verse 68 of the same chapter and say, **"Then Simon Peter answered him, Lord, to whom shall we go? thou hast the words of**

eternal life." You will never solve the problems of your life by running from them. If you get offended at work the answer is not to just find a new job, you will get offended no matter where you go. If you get offended at church, the answer is definitely not to find a new church, the answer is to fall so in love with God and His Word that His grace smoothes over any offenses that come your way. Can you not hear the people that stopped following Jesus saying, *"Well, I will find me a new church that isn't so hard on people."* Thinking of the irony of that statement makes me laugh, knowing that Jesus made them, and told them the truth because He loved them; they were offended at the Creator. I often think, if Jesus, the only perfect man, couldn't avoid offending people, I am in serious trouble.

Another thing that taking offense produces in your life is the sin of murmuring. The disciples were caught in this trap in John 6:61 it says, **"When Jesus knew in himself that his disciples murmured at it, he said unto them, Doth this offend you?"** According to the Webster's 1828 dictionary, to murmur means *"to grumble; to complain; to utter complaints in a low, half articulated voice; to utter sullen discontent; with at, before the thing which is the cause of discontent; as, murmur not at sickness; or with at or against, before the active agent which produces the evil."* You see, even the disciples were caught up in the sin of taking offense and allowed it to produce other sins in their life. God expresses His displeasure with the sin of murmuring in 1 Corinthians 10:10, saying, **"Neither murmur ye, as some of them also murmured, and were destroyed of the destroyer."** God warns us that He has destroyed others for murmuring, and commands us not to murmur. Jesus specifically says in John 6:43, **"Jesus therefore answered and said unto them, Murmur not among yourselves."** Murmuring is not just a bad habit, it is a sin that perverts our heart and turns us against God.

If we continue to take offense, it will lead us down a road further still into unforgiveness and bitterness. In Matthew 18, Jesus gives us a parable and instructions about dealing with offense in our lives. He says in verses 23-35, **"Therefore is the kingdom of heaven likened unto a certain king, which would take account of his servants. And when he had begun to reckon, one was brought unto him, which owed him ten thousand talents. But forasmuch as he had not to pay, his lord commanded him to be sold, and his wife, and children, and all that he had, and payment to be made. The servant therefore fell down, and worshipped him, saying, Lord, have patience with me, and I will pay thee all. Then the lord of that servant was moved with compassion, and loosed him, and** forgave him the debt. But the same servant went out, and found one of his fellowservants, which owed him an hundred pence: and he laid hands on him, and took him by the throat, saying, Pay me that thou owest. And his fellowservant fell down at his feet, and besought him, saying, Have patience with me, and I will pay thee all. And he would not: but went and cast him into prison, till he should pay the debt. So when his fellowservants saw what was done, they were very sorry, and came and told unto their lord all that was done. Then his lord, after that he had called him, said unto him, O thou wicked servant, I forgave thee all that debt, because thou desiredst me: Shouldest not thou also have had compassion on thy fellowservant, even as I had pity on thee? And his lord was wroth, and delivered him to the tormentors, till he should pay all that was due unto him. So likewise shall my heavenly Father do also unto you, if ye from your hearts forgive not every one his brother their trespasses." The key to understanding this passage is that God is the one that has forgiven you for your sin against Him, which is far greater than anything another person could do against you. The consequence of not forgiving our brother is that God says He will withhold forgiveness from you. I don't know about you, but the idea of God being angry at me is a far greater deterrent for me to forgive than that a man will be mad at me. Unforgiveness and bitterness gives Satan an advantage over you that you cannot overcome. 2 Corinthians 2:10-11 says, **"To whom ye forgive any thing, I *forgive* also: for if I forgave any thing, to whom I forgave *it*, for your sakes *forgave I* it in the person of Christ; Lest Satan should get an advantage of us: for we are not ignorant of his devices."** And Hebrews 12:15 says, **"Looking diligently lest any man fail of the grace of God; lest any root of bitterness springing up trouble *you*, and thereby many be defiled;"**

Seeing the causes and the consequences of taking offense, it is vital that we see the cure for it, as well. As with all problems, the cure is putting on the spiritual opposites of what causes our fleshly problems. If we are to overcome the sin of taking offense, we must begin by putting on humility. Jesus humbled Himself to come down and take on the form of a servant. Do you notice that the creator of the entire universe was willing to humble Himself for you, but Satan, a created being, was not willing to humble himself to the Creator? Many people who call themselves Christians act a whole lot more like the devil than like Jesus. They are unwilling to take on the form of a servant; they want instead for everyone to bow down at their feet and confess that they were wronged and deserved better. Biblical

humility according to the Webster's 1828 dictionary *"consists in lowliness of mind; a deep sense of one's
own unworthiness in the sight of God, self-abasement,
penitence for sin, and submission to the divine will."* In
many ways, humility can be summed up in the way
Jesus explained judgment in Matthew 7:1-5 when
He said, **"Judge not, that ye be not judged. For
with what judgment ye judge, ye shall be judged:
and with what measure ye mete, it shall be mea-
sured to you again. And why beholdest thou the
mote that is in thy brother's eye, but considerest
not the beam that is in thine own eye? Or how
wilt thou say to thy brother, Let me pull out the
mote out of thine eye; and, behold, a beam is in
thine own eye? Thou hypocrite, first cast out the
beam out of thine own eye; and then shalt thou
see clearly to cast out the mote out of thy brother's eye."** The truth is that many times the people
who take the most offense are also the biggest of-
fenders of others, and if everyone else judged them
the way that they judge they would be severely condemned which is why they feel condemned all of
the time. It is not the judgment of others; it is their
own heart judging themselves. I must first take the
beam out of my eye, and then I will see clearly the
love of God for me as well as others, and will love
them instead of judging them.

   The second step in overcoming the sin of taking

offense is to submit myself to Jesus Christ. I must become His servant. A servant has no rights, and if I am to follow Him I must give up any perceived rights I have. John 13:16 says, **"Verily, verily, I say unto you, The servant is not greater than his lord; neither he that is sent greater than he that sent him."** I must remember that Jesus did not take offense at those He was trying to minister to, even when they were crucifying Him. If I am His servant, I am to follow His example. I must cast off my feelings and rights and serve in lowliness of mind. One of the problems we have is that we live in America where we are told that we have rights, and we are always defending our rights. As a Christian, we are to surrender our rights to the Saviour and take His will on instead of our own. Ephesians 5:21 says, **"Submitting yourselves one to another in the fear of God."**

Lastly we will discuss the need to grow in Christ. If I am to overcome the sin of taking offense, I must mature in Him. I do this by adding the "Ingredients for Life" found in 2 Peter 1:5-8, which says, **"And beside this, giving all diligence, add to your faith virtue; and to virtue knowledge; And to knowledge temperance; and to temperance patience; and to patience godliness; And to godliness brotherly kindness; and to brotherly kindness charity. For if these things be in you, and abound,**

they make *you that ye shall* neither *be* barren nor unfruitful in the knowledge of our Lord Jesus Christ." This is the process of taking the stones and stumps out of the ground of my heart so that I can be a fruitful field for Him, a field that is void of offense, a field that is just usable and moldable to Him. Imagine going out into your yard to plant a garden, you get a tiller and scope out the perfect place to plant the garden, you start the tiller up and the yard yells at you, *"Hey, don't do that! I can't believe you would treat me like this! I am offended!"* This sounds crazy doesn't it? Of course, dirt has no say in where or how you plow and plant; it is up to the digression of the farmer. The farmer knows what kind of plants will grow in what kind of soil, and how to prepare the soil to grow the kind of crops he wants to grow. God in His great wisdom knows where and how to grow things in your life. He brings offense into your life to point out stones and stumps that are in the way of having a fruitful garden. 1 Peter 2:19-21 says, **"For this *is* thankworthy, if a man for conscience toward God endure grief, suffering wrongfully. For what glory *is it,* if, when ye be buffeted for your faults, ye shall take it patiently? but if, when ye do well, and suffer *for it,* ye take it patiently, this *is* acceptable with God. For even hereunto were ye called: because Christ also suffered for us, leaving us an example, that ye should follow**

his steps:" This passage shows us that God knows you will receive wrong from others when you do good, and He is interested in your response. He wants to use these situations in your life to bring Glory to Himself. Yield yourself to Him, when offenses come as they must, humble yourself to Him, submit to His Word, and grow by the experience without allowing the Devil to have a place in your life.

CHAPTER THREE

Waiting on the Lord

O f all the things in life that have been hard for me, I must say that learning to wait on the Lord has been one of the hardest. I have always been driven to accomplish things. Too often, my zeal to accomplish something has overrun my sensitivity to the Spirit of God and I have found myself alone and wondering why God wasn't helping me with this problem. After all, I did have the proper intentions. Proverbs 19:2 says, **"Also, *that* the soul *be* without knowledge, *it is* not good; and he that hasteth with *his* feet sinneth."** I have had to learn, like everyone, that neither zeal, nor good intentions, determine the will of the Lord. I have seen many people with a zeal and good intentions run head long into the trials of life, becoming bitter, many times blaming those around them for their trouble, and often even quitting serving God altogether. The Word of God has much to say about waiting on the Lord. In this chapter I want to address three primary questions: 1. "How long do I wait?" 2. "Why do I wait?"

41

and 3. "How do I wait?."

Isaiah 40:27-31 says, **"Why sayest thou, O Jacob, and speakest, O Israel, My way is hid from the LORD, and my judgment is passed over from my God? Hast thou not known? hast thou not heard,** *that* **the everlasting God, the LORD, the Creator of the ends of the earth, fainteth not, neither is weary?** *there is* **no searching of his understanding. He giveth power to the faint; and to** *them that have* **no might he increaseth strength. Even the youths shall faint and be weary, and the young men shall utterly fall: But they that wait upon the LORD shall renew** *their* **strength; they shall mount up with wings as eagles; they shall run, and not be weary;** *and* **they shall walk, and not faint."**

How long do I wait? I have asked this question many times to the Lord. *"Lord,"* I would say, *"don't you know that we don't have much time?",* as if I was the one that really knew the proper timetable for all things. I find the previous passage of scripture to be very important when it tells us that God doesn't faint or get weary. The implication here is that He does not get weary of teaching us. I have four children and I must tell you, I do sometimes get weary of teaching them things that I think they ought to already know. When we travel I tire of telling them, *"No, we are not there yet, which is why we are not get-*

ting out of the car right now." I am glad that God is much more patient with me than I am with others. When I was in eighth grade, I played for a football team. We lost our first game and really disappointed our coach. At the next practice, he lined us all up on the goal line and told us that we were to run to the other goal line and then come back, but every time he blew the whistle we were supposed to dive face first into the dirt and then jump back up. Someone had the bright idea of asking how long we were going to do this exercise and the coach evidently took offence to the question. His reply was, *"You will run until I get tired."* The bad thing about this was that all he was doing was standing blowing a whistle; we got tired a whole lot sooner than he did. Many times going through a trial I have thought Lord how long do I have to do this, only to have the reply come to my heart, *"Until you get it right. Don't worry, I'm not tired of teaching you."*

You see, God is looking for a point at which you and I become moldable to His will. The problem with impatient people is that they think they know what is best, or what needs to be done, and God wants them to let Him decide what is best. Many times I have not been given the answer and help from God that was needed until I came to the point where I said, *"I can't do this anymore."* God steps in at that point and replies, *"Good, now may-*

be you will start to listen to me." You will never learn while you are still trying to do things your way. To learn, you have to stop and be still, letting God be in control without your interference. We have story after story in sports and in military training where a leader would push his team or unit farther than they thought they could go, until they were crying out for mercy. At that point they would learn the thing that they had been missing. The teacher had tried every other way he knew how, the only thing that would work is to put them through the fire until they yielded to the lesson. Giving God the right to be in control of your life is a big step in learning to wait on the Lord. It's not just about serving Him, it is about serving Him in His time. In Ecclesiastes 3:1-8 God tells us that He has a time for everything when He says, **"To every *thing there is* a season, and a time to every purpose under the heaven: A time to be born, and a time to die; a time to plant, and a time to pluck up *that which is* planted; A time to kill, and a time to heal; a time to break down, and a time to build up; A time to weep, and a time to laugh; a time to mourn, and a time to dance; A time to cast away stones, and a time to gather stones together; a time to embrace, and a time to refrain from embracing; A time to get, and a time to lose; a time to keep, and a time to cast away; A time to rend, and a time to sew; a time**

to keep silence, and a time to speak; A time to love, and a time to hate; a time of war, and a time of peace." You see we love it when it is time to do what we want to do, but we don't want to admit that sometimes it is not God's timing for what we want to do.

Only those who finally rest on Him will receive the promise in Isaiah that He will lift them up. The promise is to those who are willing to wait upon the Lord. You and I must wait until God is through teaching us those things we need to learn. Remember, He is in charge, not you. Impatiently running your head into a door that He has not opened will produce results, but the results will be a headache for you. The sooner you yield yourself to the truth that God is in control, the happier life will be.

The second question we are going to tackle is why do I wait? God shows us eight reasons that He makes us wait through a passage in Isaiah 30:18-23 which says, "**And therefore will the LORD wait, that he may be gracious unto you, and therefore will he be exalted, that he may have mercy upon you: for the LORD is a God of judgment: blessed *are* all they that wait for him. For the people shall dwell in Zion at Jerusalem: thou shalt weep no more: he will be very gracious unto thee at the voice of thy cry; when he shall hear it, he will answer thee. And *though* the Lord give you the** bread of adversity, and the water of affliction, yet shall not thy teachers be removed into a corner any more, but thine eyes shall see thy teachers: And thine ears shall hear a word behind thee, saying, This *is* the way, walk ye in it, when ye turn to the right hand, and when ye turn to the left. Ye shall defile also the covering of thy graven images of silver, and the ornament of thy molten images of gold: thou shalt cast them away as a menstruous cloth; thou shalt say unto it, Get thee hence. Then shall he give the rain of thy seed, that thou shalt sow the ground withal; and bread of the increase of the earth, and it shall be fat and plenteous: in that day shall thy cattle feed in large pastures."

This passage shows us first of all that God has you wait so that He can be gracious to you. Grace is receiving what we do not deserve. God knows that for you to be truly thankful and recognize how gracious He is, he must allow you to suffer the pain of your own impatience sometimes. If you have been to the store anytime recently, you have probably seen a child throwing a fit about what they want. It pains me to see parents give into these little terrorists because if you give into the demands of a rebellious child, they will not be satisfied and the parent will only be sorrowful at length. God knows how to make you truly thankful and appreciative of what He gives you.

The second reason the Bible says God allows us to wait is so that He can be exalted. 1 Corinthians 10:31 says, **"Whether therefore ye eat, or drink, or whatsoever ye do, do all to the glory of God."** Everything in creation is designed to bring glory to God, our trials are to bring glory to God if we let them. The hardest thing I have had to come to grips with is the fact that God has His own plan for glorifying Himself. I begin to think, God I know what will glorify you, just let me show you. But God is much wiser than I am. Frequently I am frustrated with the way things go in life, only to find out at long reflection that God was much more glorified doing things His way than He would have been my way.

The third reason given is so that God can show you mercy. Mercy is God not giving you what you deserve. Mercy is the companion of grace and is a glorious attribute of God. You see, I deserve hell, but by His mercy, He paid my price on Calvary, and by His grace, He rose from the dead and gave me an inheritance in Heaven. 1 Peter 1:3 says, **"Blessed *be* the God and Father of our Lord Jesus Christ, which according to his abundant mercy hath begotten us again unto a lively hope by the resurrection of Jesus Christ from the dead,"**

God wants to show mercy to you. By doing so, others will see that He would show mercy to them also. Many times we fail to realize that God knows who is watching us and who will see His goodness bestowed on us. If we never come to the place of needing His mercy they would never see.

I really like the fourth reason given: so that you can be happy. The word "blessed" means "happy." God wants you to be happy and He in His providential wisdom knows that for you to be truly happy you must wait for some things. We tend to look for the temporary happy fix. As long as we are out of the situation we are currently facing, we think we will be happy. God knows true happiness, and if you will let Him, He will give it to you. The sad reality is that until you learn that real and lasting happiness is not determined by your circumstances and possessions, you will never achieve the real happiness that God wants you to have. Paul said in Philippians 4:11, **"Not that I speak in respect of want: for I have learned, in whatsoever state I am, *therewith* to be content."** Paul spent a lot of time waiting on the Lord. Because of this, he had learned that his circumstances could not determine the peace and happiness of one who was waiting on the Lord.

The fifth reason given in Isaiah 30 is so that you can learn to identify what your teachers are. Notice God did not say that He would remove them, but that by waiting you would know what they are. Your teachers are those things that you have problems with in your life. A teacher could be money, authority, or anything that brings trials into your life and makes you feel that you just have to act. As a general rule, I have learned that when I feel like I just want to take charge of a situation in life and really help God out, I should be sitting still and wait to see the salvation of God. One of the best times in my life was when I learned to wait long enough to identify what many of my teachers from God were. God has not removed them but because He has helped me identify them I do not struggle with the lessons as much. Everyone has certain areas in their life in which they are impatient. Learning what your teachers are will take the absolute frustration out of them. You will be able to identify the fact that when a problem comes up in this area, it is God working in you to perfect you. It is God in His love, making you into a more usable servant, and that is always a good thing. Job said in Job 23:10, **"But he knoweth the way that I take:** *when* **he hath tried me, I shall come forth as gold."**

The sixth reason God gives for making you wait is so that you will become sensitive to His leadership in your life. Have you ever had a puppy that you were trying to train to walk with you? You have the leash and the puppy wants to run here and run there; they get so far off that you have to gently pull them back into line. God wants you to become so sensitive to His leadership that He doesn't have to jerk you by the collar to get you back into line, but that you will stay close by Him and allow Him to lead you. Our text says, **"…thine ears shall hear a word behind thee, saying, This *is* the way, walk ye in it…"** The Bible tells us that Elijah, after winning a great victory for God, received a threat from the queen Jezebel. Instead of waiting on the Lord to deliver Him, he took off running. He ran a great way and ended up in a cave in a mountain, throwing a pity party for himself. If you haven't noticed, those parties are never very well attended. God told Elijah go out and stand in front of the cave. God made a strong wind to blow by, but the Bible tells us God wasn't in the wind. God then brought an earthquake, but He was not in the earthquake. Next, God brought a fire and it swept through the mountain, but God was not in the fire. Then an amazing thing happened: the Bible says in I Kings 19:12, **"…and after the fire a still small voice."** You see, we want God to do some great thing in order to speak to us. We want the mighty winds, the earthquakes and fires, but God wants to speak to us in the still small voice saying this is the way, walk ye in it. God will allow you to wait to teach you to be sensitive to His voice. A well trained horse does not have to have its bridle jerked to know what its master wants; it has learned to be sensitive to the tiniest motions of the master for its direction. Impatience doesn't lend itself to this type of leadership. You and I must yield ourselves to waiting on the Lord so that we will become sensitive servants to our Master.

Reason number seven God allows you to wait is so that you will rid yourself of everything but Him. Our text says, **"Ye shall defile also the covering of thy graven images of silver, and the ornament of thy molten images of gold: thou shalt cast them away as a menstruous cloth; thou shalt say unto it, Get thee hence."** God alone must have preeminence in your life; You must get rid of everything that takes His place. Sometimes things that are not necessarily wrong can take the place of God in our lives. Fishing and hunting are not evil in themselves, but if they take the place of God, they become evil in our lives. Moses one day was instructed of God to make a brass serpent and put it on a pole so that the nation of Israel could look on it and be healed from the bites of fiery serpents that had come on them. It was a beautiful picture of the fact that Jesus would be lifted up on the cross to give forgiveness and healing to all those who would call upon Him. However, this beautiful picture that God gave Moses later became a source of sin to the nation. In 2 Kings 18, Hezekiah becomes the king and does what is right before God. In verse 4 it says, **"He removed the high places, and brake the images, and cut down the groves, and brake in pieces the brasen**

serpent that Moses had made: for unto those days the children of Israel did burn incense to it: and he called it Nehushtan." That thing given of God to show them a picture of the coming Saviour had become sinful in their lives. God wants you and me to be willing to give up everything that brings a separation between us and Him.

The last reason given in our text for God allowing us to wait is so that He can bless us. You may think that this is a strange way to get blessed, but God knows how to bless you better than you think. God wants to give you the desires of your heart, but because He is good, He will only bless you when you are able to receive it, and when it won't hurt you. Proverbs 10:22 says, **"The blessing of the LORD, it maketh rich, and he addeth no sorrow with it."** This does not promise that God will make you rich with money, but that when God does bless someone it doesn't come with sorrow. I knew a man once who pulled up to church in a brand new yellow convertible. It was beautiful, he jumped out and said, *"Look what God blessed me with."* I said, *"Wow, God gave you that?"* He said, *"Well, I have pretty high payments and have had to take on a second job, but God let me get it."* Don't call your covetousness the blessing of God. When God blesses you, it won't cost. That man ended up quitting church to pay for his new god. The most frustrating thing I have faced in my life is buying something on credit and the next day someone telling me that they had felt impressed to give me what I needed. I have cost myself many blessing from God because of my impatience.

The final question we will deal with in this booklet is, how do I wait. There are four main things that we are instructed in the Bible to do while waiting on the Lord. The first is to wait in God's Word. Psalm 130:5-6 says, **"I wait for the LORD, my soul doth wait, and in his word do I hope. My soul *waiteth* for the Lord more than they that watch for the morning: *I say, more than* they that watch for the morning."** David knew that God would answer; the thing that would help him the most to be able to wait properly was to be in His Word. When you are not sure what to do, wait by reading God's Word. In His Word will He direct you. Psalm 119:105 says, **"Thy word *is* a lamp unto my feet, and a light unto my path."** God wants us to use His Word as a guide for our path, but many times we are too impatient to let God speak to us through His Word and we run out headlong into trouble because of it. God will give you direction through His Word if you will wait on Him for it. Don't fall into the trap Satan sets that says, if you don't act now, you will miss out. God has His best planned for you and if you will wait for Him you will be blessed.

The second instruction we find for waiting on

the Lord is to wait in prayer. Luke 18:1 says, **"And he spake a parable unto them *to this end,* that men ought always to pray, and not to faint;"** Someone once said that no one faints at a good time. They always faint when they should be seeking God. I can hear you now saying, *"But I did pray!"* You must remember the illustrations of prayer that Jesus gave us. He told the parable of the unjust judge in which He said that it was because the woman kept asking and asking that finally the unjust judge gave in to her request. God wants us to learn to stop relying on our own devices and come to Him instead. This is why He doesn't always answer our prayers immediately. Many people pray with a false concept. They pray, saying, *"God provide, but if you don't do it by the time I am done praying I will just put it on the credit card."* That is not waiting in prayer. Waiting in prayer means that sometimes the time you thought was important will pass so that God can test your faith in Him.

Thirdly, we must wait in belief of the goodness of God. Psalm 27:13-14 says, **"*I had fainted,* unless I had believed to see the goodness of the LORD in the land of the living. Wait on the LORD: be of good courage, and he shall strengthen thine heart: wait, I say, on the LORD."** There are many believers that can see the goodness of the Lord after death, but David said that he believed to see the goodness of the Lord in the land of the living. GOD

IS GOOD! A thousand times over and over again! David was saying, I believe that God's goodness will be shown, and I will operate my life based on that belief by waiting for Him. Romans 8:28 says, **"And we know that all things work together for good to them that love God, to them who are the called according to *his* purpose."** Now, this verse does not say that all things are good, but that God will work all things to good for the benefit of those that love Him and are called according to His purpose. Many things in life are bad, and when bad things happen, we can tend to question the goodness of God in our hearts, but we must remember that He sees the big picture and has given us a promise to work all things to our good. Remind yourself of His goodness often.

Lastly we must wait with God given expectations. Psalm 62:5 says, **"My soul, wait thou only upon God; for my expectation *is* from him."** Notice that this says my expectation is FROM Him not on Him. I have heard people say, *"Well, I expected God to do this, and He didn't."* Those are not God-given expectations. Just because you expect God to do something does not mean He is bound to do it, unless He said He would in His Word. God-given expectations are found in the Bible when God says, if you will, then I will. We are given an expectation in 2 Chronicles 7:14 that says, **"If my people, which**

are called by my name, shall humble themselves, and pray, and seek my face, and turn from their wicked ways; then will I hear from heaven, and will forgive their sin, and will heal their land." Notice this expectation comes with stipulations: if we fulfill our part then we can expect that God will fulfill His part. This is an expectation from God. Keep your expectations off of men. Men will do nothing but disappoint you if you put your expectations on them. Jeremiah 17:5 says, **"Thus saith the LORD; Cursed *be* the man that trusteth in man, and maketh flesh his arm, and whose heart departeth from the LORD."** When you take your expectations away from the Word of the Lord and put them on men, you are placing yourself under a curse. The curse is that you will have your expectations broken. Make sure that your expectations are set properly when you wait. This does not mean that you should not expect God to answer or work. We should expect that when we follow His Word, He will act according to His promises. Of this I am sure: God has never forsaken those who wait on Him. David said in Psalm 37:25, **"I have been young, and *now* am old; yet have I not seen the righteous forsaken, nor his seed begging bread."** If you will wait on the Lord, you will find the same thing to be true.

CHAPTER FOUR

Bitterness

Several years ago, after being in the ministry for just a short time, I had a foolish conflict with another pastor. The cause of this conflict is unimportant, but the result of this conflict would plague me for most of a year. Finally, God brought me to a place of seeing just how much damage I was doing to myself, both emotionally and spiritually. I praise the Lord that through His word, I was able to forsake the bitterness that had poisoned my soul. This event caused me to look at bitterness in a new way than I had before. As we explore bitterness for the next few minutes I will use my own example of struggle to try and bring forth some spiritual truths that will help others caught in this battle to free themselves from the poison of bitterness.

Hebrews 12:15 **"Looking diligently lest any man fail of the grace of God; lest any root of bitterness springing up trouble *you*, and thereby many be defiled;"** I grew up in church and in a good Christian home. Many times I have heard this

verse alluded to and preached in one form or another. Yet I failed to make the connection given in
this verse to the source of bitterness in our lives. As
you look at this verse, you see the opening warning,
**"Looking diligently lest any man fail of the grace
of God…"** Considering this statement, it is without
any reservation that I say that the grace of God has
never failed, and will never fail. That is not the basis of this statement. The point of the statement is
that you and I can fail of the grace of God. We can
fail to possess an adequate amount of God's grace to
face the trials of life. Please understand this does not
have anything to do with salvation. There are two
aspects that we will perceive of the grace of God.
First, His saving grace. God's grace is able to save all
those who call upon Him without fail, yes His grace
was, is and forever will be able to forgive all sin. The
other aspect of His grace that is significant is His
grace for living. That is to say, the grace that He gives
His children to live in this evil world. It is of that latter grace that we are in danger of falling short. James
gives an indication of how this happens when he says
in James 4:6, **"But he giveth more grace. Wherefore he saith, God resisteth the proud, but giveth
grace unto the humble."** You see two groups here,
the humble, to whom God is bestowing grace, and
the proud, whom He is resisting. I think it safe to say
that if God is able to bestow more grace upon the

humble, than that implies that He in similar fashion resists the proud by withdrawing His grace. Again, not saving grace, but grace for living. In effect, He says, OK, you think that you are really something, you think that you can handle it on your own. Well, let's see how you do without my grace to guide you through. God withdraws His grace in from our lives in areas of pride. Now remember the warning of Hebrews, "...lest any man fail of the grace of God..." When we become lifted up in pride, God withdraws His grace for living from our lives. Then when an injustice comes into our lives (it may be real or perceived), with the grace of God removed, we fall into bitterness. We are troubled and are in danger of defiling others.

Let's take a few moments and look at Jonah who I believe was a prime example of the effects of bitterness in the life of a child of God. By chapter four of Jonah, Nineveh has repented, God has forgiven them, and Jonah has rebelled again. Jonah 4:1-3 says, **"But it displeased Jonah exceedingly, and he was very angry. And he prayed unto the LORD, and said, I pray thee, O LORD, was not this my saying, when I was yet in my country? Therefore I fled before unto Tarshish: for I knew that thou *art* a gracious God, and merciful, slow to anger, and of great kindness, and repentest thee of the evil. Therefore now, O LORD, take, I**

beseech thee, my life from me; for *it is* **better for me to die than to live."** Here we find the first of five consequences to bitterness in the life of Jonah. The first consequence is that bitterness causes you to despise the forgiveness of God. Jonah couldn't believe that God would forgive the Ninevites. Some bible doubters wondered if Nineveh even existed. Then in the 1800s, British adventurer Austen Henry Layard rediscovered the lost palace and city across the Tigris River from modern day Mosul in northern Iraq.

Jonah lived during the height of the Assyrian empire. Based on the tablets excavated in Nineveh, the Assyrians were very brutal, ruthless people. They frequently raided the Northern kingdom where Jonah lived, destroying many villages and towns. The Jews hated the Ninevites. Imagine Jonah's horror when God asked him to take a message to these enemies of goodness. I can't help but picture in my mind this whole city repenting, and Jonah stomping his feet and yelling at God, *"I knew this would happen! I knew that if they heard this message they would all repent and you would forgive them! That's why I didn't want to come in the first place!"* Imagine the worst civilization today, and one preacher showing up in the heart of their most wicked city with the message of repent or God is going to destroy you. Would you have so much faith in that message that you would say the same thing as Jonah? We criticize Jonah, yet this was a man who believed God. This also was a man who was proud to be part of God's chosen people. The Jews looked down upon the Assyrian "dogs"; they were better than these uncivilized heathen. Why would God ask Jonah to take a message of repentance to people who obviously deserved to die? Why not just kill them and be done with it? Oh how great is the mercy of our God. Yet in his bitter state, Jonah despised the forgiveness that God was giving to Nineveh.

When I experienced the perceived injustice in my life I began to pray for God to judge the individual that had "wronged" me. I hope that you are more spiritual than I was, but I went so far as to suggest to God what He could do to punish the offender. I look back on this with shame; I was almost like David in his imprecatory Psalms, though operating in the flesh. I did not want God to forgive the offender; I wanted justice for myself. I was proud and wanted God to reinforce that I was right. The biggest problem with this is that when you despise God's forgiveness for someone else, you mar your own forgiveness from God. Matthew 6:15 says, **"But if ye forgive not men their trespasses, neither will your Father forgive your trespasses."** I place myself under the judgment of God, which means that I have no right to bring my petitions to the throne of God. Psalm 66:18 says, **"If I regard iniquity in my heart, the Lord will not hear *me*:"** You need to understand that when you are in bitterness, you have cut off your line of communication with God.

It is also important to know that God says in Romans 13 that vengeance belongs to Him alone. As long as you stand in front of the offender ordering God to judge them, God most likely will not. You hinder God from dealing with them because of your own pride. What a shame that our insistence on being right can hinder the work of God and bring sin into our own life.

The second consequence of bitterness is found in verses 4-5 of Jonah chapter number four: **"Then said the LORD, Doest thou well to be angry? So Jonah went out of the city, and sat on the east side of the city, and there made him a booth, and sat under it in the shadow, till he might see what would become of the city."** This consequence is that bitterness causes you to develop a singular focus on your enemy to the neglect of your own need. Imagine the city of Nineveh has repented and God has accepted, but Jonah, filled with his own sense of justice, goes out of the city, sits on the side of a hill and says, *"I am going to sit here until God comes to his senses and kills these people!"* I imagine that God may have had more things for Jonah to do, yet he was so focused on his enemy that he could not see anything else. Bitterness causes you to be spiritually blind. I remember during those dark days of my life, asking people who knew this other person, how that other person was doing, but only to find out if God had started the judgment yet. I inwardly longed to hear bad things were happening to them. It is amazing as I have met and dealt with others that are in the gall of bitterness just how singularly focused they are. Their whole life seems to pivot on a singular event or relationship. Often the other party is oblivious to this and lives a normal life, while these pine away in sorrow. Someone once said that bitterness is a pill you swallow hoping someone else will die. Yet, it is you who will suffer, ignoring all the good things of your life, laboring under the false pretence that if God did judge them that it would somehow vindicate you and make you feel better. You have succumbed to a lie.

The third consequence of bitterness is found in the next couple of verses. Jonah 4:6-8 **"And the LORD God prepared a gourd, and made *it* to come up over Jonah, that it might be a shadow over his head, to deliver him from his grief. So Jonah was exceeding glad of the gourd. But God prepared a worm when the morning rose the next day, and it smote the gourd that it withered. And it came to pass, when the sun did arise, that God prepared a vehement east wind; and the sun**

beat upon the head of Jonah, that he fainted, and wished in himself to die, and said, *It is* better for me to die than to live." This consequence is evident to everyone but the infected: pettiness. I have yet to meet a bitter person that isn't petty. I have been in church my whole life, but I have only seen one church split that was over doctrine. I was recently told that doctrine divides not among churches. No, it is the color of the carpet, the decorations in the bathroom, the plants in the entryway…the list goes on and on and all boils down to one thing, pettiness. Every preacher could give you a number of examples of the petty things people have done to others in the church because of bitterness.

Bitter people do things out of spite. Here sits Jonah, the recipient of God's mercy, both spiritually and now physically. He is sheltered in his bitterness by a gourd. How thankful he is for the gourd. And yet as God shows a picture of what bitterness really is to Jonah, a worm that eats at your insides until you die, he gets angry at God again. Bitter people frequently get angry at those who try to help them out of the pit they are in. I am justified to feel this way, they say. If you would have suffered what I did you would feel the same way. Can you hear Jonah crying for the gourd, that petty little thing that was given to help him see his folly? It was unsettling to God to hear him cry over a gourd and at the same time wish death upon hundreds of thousands of people. My own pettiness was manifest in the fact that I decided to warn the object of my bitterness in a letter of the impending doom of God upon him. After God showed me my wickedness, I couldn't believe that I would do such a wicked thing. If you and I received the just reward for our sins, God would strike us down right this minute. Yet we have a compassionate, longsuffering God. He was with me, in bringing me through His word to a place of forgiveness.

The fourth consequence is somewhat prophesied in Proverbs 13:12 **"Hope deferred maketh the heart sick: but *when* the desire cometh, *it is* a tree of life."** While the judgment of those you are bitter against will not bring a tree of life into your heart, the deferred hope of their judgment will make your heart sick, and you will eventually sink into depression just as Jonah did in Jonah 4:9, **"And God said to Jonah, Doest thou well to be angry for the gourd? And he said, I do well to be angry, *even* unto death."** Maybe you have thought the same thing concerning your bitterness: I do well to be angry until I die. Depression is rarely an organic physical problem or one that is unrelated to emotional issues. It is caused most often by sin. Here Jonah looks in the face of God and says in effect I will not get right. Be careful, there is a line you can cross with God. 1 John 5:16, **"If any man see his** brother sin a sin *which is* not unto death, he shall ask, and he shall give him life for them that sin not unto death. There is a sin unto death: I do not say that he shall pray for it." When you come to the place that you tell God you will not get right you are in danger of crossing a deadline with God. God is very longsuffering and gives us many opportunities to turn but there is a point in which He stops you from harming others. I praise God that He pulled me out of this mess before I came to this point, but I have met many who did not get right. They fell into depression; the world told them it was because they didn't like themselves enough. The truth is that many times it is the opposite: they liked themselves too much. They are many times prideful and do not believe that they deserve the treatment that they are receiving from others and God, thus they fall into depression. You can still be salvaged even if you have gotten this far. It is not yet too late for you to be restored to the truth. The answer is not drugs though, the answer is the Bible. In just a few minutes we will address a specific answer for you.

The last consequence is unstated, yet I believe is implied and born out by historical facts. Jonah 4:10-11 says, **"Then said the LORD, Thou hast had pity on the gourd, for the which thou hast not laboured, neither madest it grow; which came up in a night, and perished in a night: And should** not I spare Nineveh, that great city, wherein are more than sixscore thousand persons that cannot discern between their right hand and their left hand; and *also* much cattle?" Just a little distance from Nineveh is a mosque that claims to be the burial place of Jonah. The scripture is devoid of a further mention of the life of Jonah. The last time we see him is sitting on the side of the hill in bitterness asking God to kill him for the third time. I believe the last consequence of bitterness is death. First spiritual, than physical. The fact that you are reading this is a sign that you still have a chance to get things right, to avoid this final consequence. But how? The answer to that is found where we started just a few pages back.

If the Bible is right, the source of bitterness is a failure of the grace of God, and that failure is caused by God's grace being withdrawn from the proud. It only stands to reason that you must humble yourself to receive the grace of God to cover this sin. James 4:7-9 gives a three step process to humbling one's self. **"Submit yourselves therefore to God. Resist the devil, and he will flee from you. Draw nigh to God, and he will draw nigh to you. Cleanse *your* hands, *ye* sinners; and purify *your* hearts, *ye* double minded. Be afflicted, and mourn, and weep: let your laughter be turned to mourning, and *your* joy to heaviness."** The first step in the process of humbling yourself is to submit to God your thinking and feelings. Surrender your right to feel anger and bitterness, admit that your thinking has not solved the problem. Your thinking and feelings have magnified the problem and must be surrendered to His thinking and feelings. 2 Corinthians 2:10-11 says, **"To whom ye forgive any thing, I *forgive* also: for if I forgave any thing, to whom I forgave *it*, for your sakes *forgave I it* in the person of Christ; Lest Satan should get an advantage of us: for we are not ignorant of his devices."** Paul implies here that the only way to forgive anyone is to do so through yielding your thinking and feelings to Christ. You may have tried to forgive the person in the past; it could be that you even have punished yourself for not being a good enough Christian to stop feeling and thinking the way you do about them. The answer is that you cannot do it through your own power. As Paul looked on those who had wronged him (and they were many) he pictured Jesus on the cross. As He was on the cross, He was looking down through time and saw every sin that would be committed, and His choice on the cross was to forgive each and every one of them, even the ones that would be committed against you. Paul chose to stop going by his own thinking and feelings and make a conscience choice to go by Christ's. Forgiveness is a choice, not a feeling. This choice begins with the first step of humbling yourself and submitting your thinking and feelings to God. Submit your wounded heart and spirit, and it will amaze you how quickly He can heal it.

The second step in this humbling process is that of resisting the Devil and drawing nigh to God. The act of resisting is summed up in the act of drawing nigh. You cannot resist the Devil by your own power, but as you draw nigh to God, the Devil must flee. One of my favorite illustrations of the Father's response to us is the prodigal son. I have heard it said it is just as far back to the house as it was when you left. This may be true, but it is not as far back to the Father. The Bible tells us that the Father was watching and when he saw His son a great way off He ran to meet him. James reinforces this thought when he says draw nigh to God, and He will draw nigh to you. Every step you take toward God is equal to two. The blessed thing about the story is that the son was in the Fathers embrace long before he reached the house; it was the Father that ultimately brought the son back to the house.

The Bible tells us that the Devil is limited in where he can go, and what he can do by the Father. The Devil must keep a certain distance from God, as you draw nigh to Him, the Devil must flee. How do you draw nigh to God? The answer is basic: through prayer, Bible reading, and church attendance. You may say you have been doing those things and it hasn't worked. No, you have been doing those things while filled with pride and being resisted by the Father. You may have been doing the right things, but with the wrong spirit, God was pushing you away. Once you come in a humbled spirit, you will find the Father responds differently to you. Look at these verses: Psalm 34:18 **"The LORD *is* nigh unto them that are of a broken heart; and saveth such as be of a contrite spirit."** Psalm 51:17 **"The sacrifices of God *are* a broken spirit: a broken and a contrite heart, O God, thou wilt not despise."** Isaiah 57:15 **"For thus saith the high and lofty One that inhabiteth eternity, whose name *is* Holy; I dwell in the high and holy *place*, with him also *that* is of a contrite and humble spirit, to revive the spirit of the humble, and to revive the heart of the contrite ones."** Humility is precious in the sight of God, He wants to receive you but you must come on His terms.

The third step in humbling yourself is what is listed in the last of James 4:8-9 **"...Cleanse *your* hands, *ye* sinners; and purify *your* hearts, *ye* double minded. Be afflicted, and mourn, and weep: let your laughter be turned to mourning, and *your* joy to heaviness."** To humble yourself and receive the grace of God back on your life, you must confess that you have been in sin. God is not as concerned with the offence as your response to it. You have sinned; you have been in unforgiveness and bitterness. It must be confessed for what it is: SIN. We have a tendency to justify and rename sin to make it sound more acceptable, but God will have none of it. If you want healing, you must call it what God does, and you must be sorry for it. Not sorry for what it has done to you, but sorry for what you have done to a just, holy, and righteous God.

Let's take a minute to address those who have possibly slipped as far into bitterness as depression. The Bible answer for you is to begin to look for things to praise God for. Start by setting your expectations in God instead of man as David said in Psalm 62:5, **"My soul, wait thou only upon God; for my expectation *is* from him."** Then apply Isaiah 61:3 **"To appoint unto them that mourn in Zion, to give unto them beauty for ashes, the oil of joy for mourning, the garment of praise for the spirit of heaviness; that they might be called trees of righteousness, the planting of the LORD, that he might be glorified."** Praise to God raises the spirit of man. Begin to make lists of things that you can see and think of to praise God for. Do so audibly, the Devil does not like to hear the praises of God, but the habit of praising God with your mouth will draw you up out of depression.

Back to James, I love verse ten of James 4 which

says, **"Humble yourselves in the sight of the Lord, and he shall lift you up."** He will lift you up out of pride, bitterness, depression, you name it, He will lift you up when you follow the Biblical recipe for humility.

One last thing that I wish to address is what happened to me when I finally gave the issue of my bitterness over to God. Suddenly it dawned on me how sinful I had been, I remembered the prayers and wishes for God to judge the other individual. I was crushed by this. I began to beg God to forgive them as well, not to judge them. My heart became heavy, I sought their forgiveness for holding bitterness against them. To this day I pray for them frequently, that God would bless them. When your heart is right, you will not desire the judgment of God upon others; you will desire them to receive the same mercy that you received undeservingly. What joy it is to pray for God to bless others rather than curse them. This must have been how the author felt when he wrote in Psalm 133:1 **"Behold, how good and how pleasant *it is* for brethren to dwell together in unity!"** Please, I ask you to heed the warning of the Scriptures as to the destructive nature of bitterness! If you are ensnared by it, follow these Biblical steps to overcome this trap of the Devil. You are not ignorant of his devises. Peace and joy await you when you humble yourself.

CHAPTER FIVE

Anxiety

In 1993, my wife and I were sent out of the Hoxie Baptist Temple in Hoxie, KS, to go and start a church in Oberlin, KS. It was an exciting time in our lives. After just about 6 months, God had given us a building that we were remodeling, and we were running twenty eight on Sunday mornings. We had a young man come out with "the desire to help us" after a few months of his help, we had a church walk out. We had twenty eight one Sunday and two the next. I was thankful that my wife stayed. I was devastated. I began to experience severe anxiety. I was so nervous all the time that I was unable to keep down food for several months. I had never experienced this before. I had trouble sleeping, and couldn't shake the feeling that the world was falling in around me. You may be experiencing some of the same symptoms that I did. At the time, I didn't know how to deal with the problem Biblically. Thankfully, God brought me through the incident.

The Bible does give an answer as to how to deal

with anxiety. It is with great assurance that I tell you that you do not have to live with the problem of anxiety. God has peace for you and the Scripture provides a step-by-step solution that if you put it into practice you can live free from fear. Anxiety is defined by the Webster's 1828 dictionary as concern respecting some event, which disturbs the mind, and keeps it in a state of painful uneasiness. It involves suspense respecting an event, and often a perplexity of mind to know how to shape our conduct. It is important when you look at a problem to define it in the way that the scriptures do. The Bible use several words to describe anxiety such as "careful", that is, being full of care over something. It also uses the words troubled, doubtful, take thought, and fret. These words describe different aspects of what we commonly call anxiety. Let's begin our look at this topic by examining what some of the spiritual results of anxiety are.

One of the first things the Bible tells us anxiety brings is found in Luke 12:22-24. **"And he said unto his disciples, Therefore I say unto you, Take no thought for your life, what ye shall eat; neither for the body, what ye shall put on. The life is more than meat, and the body *is more* than raiment. Consider the ravens: for they neither sow nor reap; which neither have storehouse nor barn; and God feedeth them: how much** more are ye better than the fowls?" This passage shows us that anxiety is directly related to a lack of faith. Maybe you have never doubted God's ability to work, but have you doubted His willingness to work for you? I have heard people say before, *"I know God can, I am just not sure He will for me."* This lack of faith hinders God's answering your prayers. It says in James 1:6-8, **"But let him ask in faith, nothing wavering. For he that wavereth is like a wave of the sea driven with the wind and tossed. For let not that man think that he shall receive any thing of the Lord. A double minded man *is* unstable in all his ways."** It isn't that God doesn't want to answer your prayers, and meet your needs, it is your lack of faith that hinders Him.

The next thing that anxiety brings is a lack of vision. Luke 10:38-42 says, **"Now it came to pass, as they went, that he entered into a certain village: and a certain woman named Martha received him into her house. And she had a sister called Mary, which also sat at Jesus' feet, and heard his word. But Martha was cumbered about much serving, and came to him, and said, Lord, dost thou not care that my sister hath left me to serve alone? bid her therefore that she help me. And Jesus answered and said unto her, Martha, Martha, thou art careful and troubled about many things: But one thing is needful: and Mary hath**

chosen that good part, which shall not be taken away from her." Martha was **"careful and troubled"** Jesus said. Her anxiety took away the vision that Mary saw, that of the joy of sitting at the feet of Jesus. Anxiety often causes a singular focus on a problem to the neglect of all the other gifts of God in your life. Anxiety over one thing can steal your joy in all others. Many times those involved in the work of the Lord can find themselves with the same problem as Martha, we are in the same room as the Lord, and yet our hearts are far from Him. We allow ourselves to be **"...careful and troubled about many things:"** and forget that one thing that is needful. How to get back to that one needful thing is what we will address in just a little bit.

Then we find in Romans 14:23 **"And he that doubteth is damned if he eat, because *he eateth* not of faith: for whatsoever *is* not of faith is sin."** Anxiety is operating without faith, which is sin. It separates you from God. It is unfortunate that it is one of those things that can become so familiar to the heart that a person can almost feel awkward not being anxious. It becomes a personality trait and we excuse it as such saying *"that is just how I am,"* instead of acknowledging that it is sin and contrary to God.

The last thing we are going to look at concerning what anxiety brings is found in Psalm 37:1. **"Fret**

not thyself because of evildoers, neither be thou envious against the workers of iniquity." If we are not careful, anxiety can cause us to be envious of those who do evil. You may look around and think, *"Those people who just do their own thing and don't have to worry about serving the Lord or giving or living for Him, that is the way to avoid this anxiety."* God says in the next verse there, *"For they shall soon be cut down like the grass, and wither as the green herb."* You see that "grass is greener" thinking is just wrong. They have more problems than you can see. They are trying to face the same problems you are, only without God to aid them. By the Word of God, we know that all men have troubles, and the greatest of these troubles is going to be reserved for those who are without God after this life. Do not be envious of evil doers.

Next let's look at some of the physical and emotional results of anxiety. As I was sitting in Bible college one day, the teacher said, *"90% of the things that people worry about never happen."* Now I have a tendency to look at things somewhat differently, so I said that this proved that worry works. You see either it is totally worthless, or it is 90% effective. Well, I think that we all know the truth, it is totally worthless. Your anxiety and worry has never changed the outcome of one event. It has, however, changed you. It has brought you emotional instability. James 1:8 says, **"A double minded man *is* unstable in all his ways."** Anxious people frequently have difficulty making simple decisions. They become double-minded, they struggle with being insecure emotionally.

Anxious people are also quite stressed out. I have heard many doctors and nurses confirm the statement that 80% of all illness is caused by stress. As you stress out, your body tenses up and your organs stop producing the chemicals you need to have healthy function. I know many who have shingles and hives that have been told it is because of stress. Heart attacks and a whole list of other ailments are often attributed to stress. Anxious people are stressful people. Many times anxious people stress over things that everyone else sees as a little problem, and truthfully, if it was someone else, you would probably call it a little problem, as well. We tend to treat problems like surgery, the only minor surgery is the one happening to someone else, and the only minor problem is the one someone else is having. Matthew 11:29 says, **"Take my yoke upon you, and learn of me; for I am meek and lowly in heart: and ye shall find rest unto your souls."** Doctors will tell you that the cure for stress is to rest; the true cure is to rest in the Lord.

So with anxiety causing all of these problems within our lives, where do we find an answer? I can tell you that the answer is not in the latest drug that is on the market. No, the answer is found in Psalm 37:3-5. **"Trust in the LORD, and do good;** *so* **shalt thou dwell in the land, and verily thou shalt be fed. Delight thyself also in the LORD; and he shall give thee the desires of thine heart. Commit thy way unto the LORD; trust also in him; and he shall bring** *it* **to pass."** There are four things listed in this passage that David used to overcome anxiety himself. These four things produce the antidote that is needed to exterminate the poison of anxiety. Let's examine them each beginning with the first statement made in verse three.

Trust in the Lord. At first glance you may say, *"I have trusted in the Lord. I have accepted the Lord, and I even try to live by faith."* However, if you are troubled by anxiety, the first thing that you have to face up to is that you have a lack of trust in the Lord. Romans 10:17 gives an answer to increasing your trust in the Lord. It says, **"So then faith** *cometh* **by hearing, and hearing by the word of God."** Sometimes the Scriptures are so simple, we pass right over the truth that they convey. If you want to increase your faith or trust in the Lord, you must hear the word of God. If you will get a copy of the Bible on tape or CD and play it on a regular basis, you will begin to increase your trust in the Lord. Don't take my word for it, just accept God's. I have heard many concepts on how to increase your faith, yet God couldn't have been any more plain. 1 Peter 2:2 tells us, **"As new-born babes, desire the sincere milk of the word, that ye may grow thereby:"** He is not only talking to babies, but to those who have grown in Christ, as well, yet the admonition is the same, desire the Word and it will cause you to grow. There is a danger that we will treat the Word with less and less significance as we are longer in Christ. It can become familiar; we think that we have heard it before and already have a predisposed idea of what it says. Yet we are to hear it as if for the first time. We are to listen to it as though we had never heard. This hunger and longing after the Word of God allows the Holy Spirit to minister faith to our souls as we grow through the Word. I am amazed that even though I have been saved now almost twenty-six years, there have been times that I have read my Bible out of duty rather than love. When I read it out of love, I often see things that I had missed before. How wonderful it is to see the scriptures in a fresh way, the excitement of God speaking to my soul never gets old. Immerse yourself in the Word of God. Read it, listen to it, hear it preached, and it will increase your faith.

The second statement is quite short yet carries a great deal of power. It simply says "do good." One of the problems that anxiety creates is a "me" mentality. Everything becomes about you, how will this affect me, how will I deal with this. The problem is that you are too concerned about you. I have had people tell me, *"I am worried about what everyone thinks about me."* How arrogant! They probably aren't thinking about you at all. They are probably thinking about what everyone else thinks about them, as well. James 1:27 says, **"Pure religion and undefiled before God and the Father is this, To visit the fatherless and widows in their affliction, *and* to keep himself unspotted from the world."** To do good is to serve others, and to do so out of pure religion is to serve those who cannot serve you back. Paul exhorts us many times to good works, such as in Titus 3:14, **"And let ours also learn to maintain good works for necessary uses, that they be not unfruitful."** Doing good for others is a Biblical method of getting your mind off of all your problems. Frequently when you serve others, you find that they have worse problems than yourself. To exhort others to trust the Lord and then not to do so yourself would be foolish. I have encouraged people to do many things in service to others. You may spend time at a local nursing facility just talking to those who have no one else. Maybe you know someone who is homebound and needs company or assistance around the house. It could be for someone who is going through a tough time financially. I believe that this service should be done as anonymously as possible to allow the glory to go to God. My father quoted a song many times as I was growing up titled "Others." It said in part, *"Help me to live from day to day, in such a self forgetful way, that even when I kneel to pray, my prayer shall be for others. Others Lord, yes, others, let this my motto be. Help me to live for others, that I might live like thee."* The Christian life that is self focused is not in line with the will of God. It should be centered on serving others. This is the example of our Saviour. This explains why He said to take His yoke upon us. His yoke is service, not self-contemplation. His yoke is giving, not taking our burdens upon ourselves. When we give ourselves to doing good, He takes up our struggles and carries them for us.

The third step in overcoming anxiety is found in verse four of our text, **"Delight thyself also in the LORD…."** David repeatedly told us that he delighted himself in the law of the Lord. Look at these passages: Psalm 1:2 **"But his delight *is* in the law of the LORD; and in his law doth he meditate day and night."** Psalm 119:16 **"I will delight myself in thy statutes: I will not forget thy word."** Psalm 119:24 **"Thy testimonies also *are* my delight *and* my counsellors."** Psalm 119:35 **"Make me to go in the path of thy commandments; for therein do I delight."** Psalm 119:47 **"And I will delight my-**

self in thy commandments, which I have loved." Psalm 119:70 "Their heart is as fat as grease; *but* I delight in thy law." Psalm 119:77 "Let thy tender mercies come unto me, that I may live: for thy law *is* my delight." Psalm 119:174 "I have longed for thy salvation, O LORD; and thy law *is* my delight." Paul also said this in Romans 7:22 "For I delight in the law of God after the inward man:" It is clear from the scriptures that the first step to delighting in the Lord is to delight in His Word. The Webster's 1828 dictionary has this statement about the word delight, *"Delight is a more permanent pleasure than joy, and not dependent on sudden excitement."* This delighting in the Lord is not due to accident, it is a purposed direction, a choice of life. David says in Psalm 40:8 "I delight to do thy will, O my God: yea, thy law *is* within my heart." Most things in life are a choice; it is not God's will for us to leave our lives up to the winds that blow. We are to choose to be what He desires us to be. In that choosing, we must put those things around us that cause us to see how good it is to delight in Him. Being thankful and keeping lists of things to be thankful for is an excellent way to delight yourself in the Lord.

The fourth step addressed in Psalm 37 is in verse five where it says, "Commit thy way unto the Lord..." Committing your way to the Lord is two-fold. First, there is the part of doing everything that

God has already told you to do in His Word. David said in Psalm 119:105, **"Thy word *is* a lamp unto my feet, and a light unto my path."** Many times anxiety in the life of a Christian is directly related to disobeying a direct instruction in the Scriptures. Examine your path. Are you being obedient to what you know that the Bible has commanded you to do? Joshua 1:8 says, **"This book of the law shall not depart out of thy mouth; but thou shalt meditate therein day and night, that thou mayest observe to do according to all that is written therein: for then thou shalt make thy way prosperous, and then thou shalt have good success."** Did you catch the part of that verse that says when you observe all that is written in His Word that you would reap the rewards? Most people obey as much as they want to, but they have drawn a line that God is not allowed to cross in their lives. These are areas that they place off-limits to God. Do you have such areas? If so, it could be the reason you do not have freedom from anxiety is that you have not yet committed every way to the Lord.

The second part of committing your way unto the Lord is taking each decision to the Lord. Proverbs 3:5-6 says, **"Trust in the LORD with all thine heart; and lean not unto thine own understanding. In all thy ways acknowledge him, and he shall direct thy paths."** Often we go to God in prayer only when we run out of our own thoughts. As long as you believe that you are wise enough to run your own life, you will continue to face the anxiety of those decisions. The Bible tells us that we are not capable of running our own lives in Jeremiah 10:23. **"O LORD, I know that the way of man *is* not in himself: *it is* not in man that walketh to direct his steps."** Our decisions must be based either on direct instruction from God's Word, or filtered through prayer. This is why 1 Thessalonians 5:17 says, **"Pray without ceasing."** Philippians 4:6 tells us, **"Be careful for nothing; but in every thing by prayer and supplication with thanksgiving let your requests be made known unto God."** Remember careful is a Bible word meaning full of care or anxious. Instead of being full of care, we are to pray and commit our way unto the Lord.

How wonderful it is to see the promises in the Word of God that accompany these four steps to eliminating anxiety. Psalm 37:3 promises, **"...*so* shalt thou dwell in the land, and verily thou shalt be fed."** Here God promises possession and provision for those who trust in Him and do good. Jesus reinforced this in Matthew 6:25-34. **"Therefore I say unto you, Take no thought for your life, what ye shall eat, or what ye shall drink; nor yet for your body, what ye shall put on. Is not the life more than meat, and the body than raiment? Be-**

hold the fowls of the air: for they sow not, neither do they reap, nor gather into barns; yet your heavenly Father feedeth them. Are ye not much better than they? Which of you by taking thought can add one cubit unto his stature? And why take ye thought for raiment? Consider the lilies of the field, how they grow; they toil not, neither do they spin: And yet I say unto you, That even Solomon in all his glory was not arrayed like one of these. Wherefore, if God so clothe the grass of the field, which to day is, and to morrow is cast into the oven, *shall he* not much more *clothe* you, O ye of little faith? Therefore take no thought, saying, What shall we eat? or, What shall we drink? or, Wherewithal shall we be clothed? (For after all these things do the Gentiles seek:) for your heavenly Father knoweth that ye have need of all these things. But seek ye first the kingdom of God, and his righteousness; and all these things shall be added unto you. Take therefore no thought for the morrow: for the morrow shall take thought for the things of itself. Sufficient unto the day *is* the evil thereof." If your anxiety is primarily over your possessions and provision, then you should focus a lot on the aspects of trusting the Lord and doing good. The promises for these things follow those instructions.

Psalm 37:4 promises, "... and he shall give thee

the desires of thine heart." This promise comes after telling you to delight yourself in Him. James 4:1-3 says, "**From whence *come* wars and fightings among you? *come they* not hence, *even* of your lusts that war in your members? Ye lust, and have not: ye kill, and desire to have, and cannot obtain: ye fight and war, yet ye have not, because ye ask not. Ye ask, and receive not, because ye ask amiss, that ye may consume *it* upon your lusts.**" The truth is that when you delight yourself in the Lord, the desires of your heart will change. Your desires will no longer be after your lusts, but they will be after His will. When you desire His will, He is willing to give it to you. If you have a problem being anxious over things you desire to have, you should center a lot of your attention in the action of delighting in the Lord.

Psalm 37:5 tells us that if we commit our way to Him, "**... and he shall bring *it* to pass.**" If your anxiety stems from being uncertain over what will happen in the future, or upon certain events, then you need to commit your way unto Him. The problem is that you continue to take control back from God, when you do not have the ability to run your life. Psalm 37:6 follows this passage and says, "**And he shall bring forth thy righteousness as the light, and thy judgment as the noonday.**" When you do these things to overcome anxiety, God's righteousness will shine in you as never before. Your judgment will be clear, you will be able to make the right decisions, and expect the right outcomes because you are depending on Him and not on yourself. Philippians 4:7 promises that if you commit your way to God, **"And the peace of God, which passeth all understanding, shall keep your hearts and minds through Christ Jesus."**

All through the Scriptures God has given us the answer for the problems that we face in life. I hope that you have found an answer for the problems that you struggle with.

CHAPTER SIX

Freedom

*Biblical steps to breaking the power
of sin in the life of a Christian.*

As a Christian I struggled with sins that dominated my life for years. I felt as though I could never gain the victory, and may be doomed to spend a lifetime suffering under the weight of the sins in my life. I heard messages many times saying, *"Leave it on the altar."* Though this sounds very spiritual, I found that no one could tell me exactly how that worked. It wasn't for lack of desire, repentance, or desperation. Finally, I came to the point that I begged God, *"If I can't be delivered, please take me out of this world."* This may sound extreme to some, but I found that many people have come to the same place in life. Many people who sit in church every service have all but given up hope that there is any way for them to be delivered from the feeling of bondage to their sin. Satan has been successful in stealing the heart out of many who truly desire to serve God yet feel that because of sin in their life they are doomed to suffer for the rest of their lives. It seems that nearly

weekly you hear of people who have been seem-
ingly loyal servants of God, pastors, missionaries,
deacons, teachers, and faithful lay people, who have
been discovered to be in some form of devastating
sin. These are not isolated incidents. Our churches
are largely anemic due to the sin that is engulfing
the lives of Christians, from the pew to the pulpit.
After years of searching, God opened his word to
me in a way that I had never seen before. The things
contained in this chapter are not new; they are Biblical. As you read through this chapter I challenge
you to search the scriptures to see if these things be
so. Do not take my word for it; let the word of God
speak for itself.

Mark 9:17-29 says, **"And one of the multitude
answered and said, Master, I have brought unto
thee my son, which hath a dumb spirit; And
wheresoever he taketh him, he teareth him: and
he foameth, and gnasheth with his teeth, and
pineth away: and I spake to thy disciples that
they should cast him out; and they could not.
He answereth him, and saith, O faithless generation, how long shall I be with you? how long
shall I suffer you? bring him unto me. And they
brought him unto him: and when he saw him,
straightway the spirit tare him; and he fell on the
ground, and wallowed foaming. And he asked
his father, How long is it ago since this came**

unto him? And he said, Of a child. And ofttimes it hath cast him into the fire, and into the waters, to destroy him: but if thou canst do any thing, have compassion on us, and help us. Jesus said unto him, If thou canst believe, all things are possible to him that believeth. And straightway the father of the child cried out, and said with tears, Lord, I believe; help thou mine unbelief. When Jesus saw that the people came running together, he rebuked the foul spirit, saying unto him, *Thou* dumb and deaf spirit, I charge thee, come out of him, and enter no more into him. And *the spirit* cried, and rent him sore, and came out of him: and he was as one dead; insomuch that many said, He is dead. But Jesus took him by the hand, and lifted him up; and he arose. And when he was come into the house, his disciples asked him privately, Why could not we cast him out? And he said unto them, This kind can come forth by nothing, but by prayer and fasting."

In this passage, the disciples were faced with a spiritual battle: the deliverance of a young man over the power of satanic forces. Though they did everything they knew to do, they failed in casting out the spirit that possessed the boy. After gaining deliverance for the child, Jesus admonished the disciples that there are some spiritual battles that cannot be won except with prayer and fasting. We are in a spiritual battle, and it is imperative that we recognize the struggle with sin as such. 2 Corinthians 10:3-6 says, **"For though we walk after the flesh, we do not war after the flesh: (For the weapons of our warfare *are* not carnal, but mighty through God to the pulling down of strong holds;) Casting down imaginations, and every high thing that exalteth itself against the knowledge of God, and bringing into captivity every thought to the obedience of Christ; And having in a readiness to revenge all disobedience, when your obedience is fulfilled."** This passage gives us some important facts concerning this spiritual warfare in which we are engaged. Four of these facts are key to our understanding of this subject, and are listed here in order found in the passage.

1. We have spiritual weapons. What they are and how to use them will be discussed later in this chapter.

2. These spiritual weapons are for the purpose of breaking down strongholds.

3. These strongholds are in the mind. The battlefield of the Christian life is in the mind. Verse 5 says, **"Casting down imaginations... and bringing into captivity every thought..."**

4. There is a way to revenge all disobedience according to verse 6.

For clarity of understanding, we are going to

examine in depth these things in a different order, beginning with a look at the strongholds. In our society, we call strongholds addiction, or compulsion. These things may be any multitude of sins. We all have a propensity toward a different sin. One person may take a drink of liquor, and never become a drunk; another may view a piece of pornography and not feel a strong desire to indulge in this sin. Yet all men have a tendency toward a particular sin. Proverbs 5:22 says, **"His own iniquities shall take the wicked himself, and he shall be holden with the cords of his sin."** The Bible doesn't use the term addiction in reference to sin, but it does use the terms strongholds and cords. The devastating part of these sins is that the person seems to be out of control, that they feel that they have no power to control the sin. 2 Timothy 2:26 says, **"And *that* they may recover themselves out of the snare of the devil, who are taken captive by him at his will."** Notice that according to this scripture, there are some that can be taken captive by the devil at his will, not theirs. How is it possible that the devil could have this power over men? When you apply the verses in second Corinthians and Proverbs to this verse, it is easy to see that when we sin we attach spiritual cords of sin.

When you first get involved in sin, you think you are in control, but every time you take part in that sin, you are tying a cord around yourself. Satan is at the other end of that cord, and he knows he can pull your cord any time and cause you trouble. The more cords you attach by participating in that sin, the stronger the pull gets, and the more cords Satan can pull to draw you back into sin. The way to overcome this sin is to cut all the cords so that there is nothing for the devil to pull you with.

These are strongholds of sin that are known and used by the devil. Many people will say, "It is like I feel a tugging in my gut. I don't want to commit the sin, but the feeling gets stronger and stronger until I cannot withstand it any longer." They are being taken captive by the devil at his will. Others have said, *"I was on my way to the place where I would commit the sin, and all the while I was praying, 'Lord, please stop me from committing this sin again. Let me have an accident, or something that would stop me.'"* They are being taken captive by the devil at his will. Some will say a Christian could never be affected this way; however while talking to Christians who have a profession of faith, the author of Hebrews 10:26 says, **"For if we sin willfully after that we the knowledge of the truth, there remained no more sacrifice for sins,"** The Christian who commits willful sin will suffer punishment here on earth for that sin. Paul even says in reference to a young man who was living in sin in the church of Corinth, in 1 Corinthians 5:5, **"To deliver such an one unto Satan for the destruction of the flesh, that the spirit may be saved in the day of the Lord Jesus."** Much time is spent in the New Testament dealing with staying out of the clutches of sin. We are warned in Ephesians 6 to put on the whole armor of God that we may be able to stand against the whiles of the devil, and in James 4:7 we are admonished, **"Submit yourselves therefore to God. Resist the devil, and he will flee from you."** Much emphasis is placed on the aspect of resisting the devil, however the key to this very action is found in drawing nigh to God. 1 Peter 5:8-9 says, **"Be sober, be vigilant; because your adversary the devil, as a roaring lion, walketh about, seeking whom he may devour: Whom resist steadfast in the faith, knowing that the same afflictions are accomplished in your brethren that are in the world."** What are the same afflictions that are in the world? The answer is painfully obvious: we struggle with the sin that tries to dominate our lives, and with Satan who tries to take us captive by the cords of sin which we have attached.

The more you participate in sin, the more you get tangled up by it and the cords overwhelm you until you believe there is no hope of getting free. You feel you are doomed to fight this forever, and many people give in and stop fighting. Even Christians can be entangled in these sins.

2 Peter 2:18-20 **"For when they speak great swelling *words* of vanity, they allure through the lusts of the flesh, *through much* wantonness, those that were clean escaped from them who live in error. While they promise them liberty, they themselves are the servants of corruption: for of whom a man is overcome, of the same is he brought in bondage. For if after they have escaped the pollutions of the world through the knowledge of the Lord and Saviour Jesus Christ, they are again entangled therein, and overcome, the latter end is worse with them than the beginning."**

Some people live their lives in denial of the power of sin. It is true that we as Christians have been delivered from the power of sin which sends a man to hell, and it is also true that we have deliverance from abiding in sin as a lifestyle, if we know how to claim the promise. Colossians 1:13 says, **"Who hath delivered us from the power of darkness, and hath translated *us* into the kingdom of his dear Son:"** The great truth of the Bible on this topic is that we do not have to be in bondage. The sad reality is that too many are, and they do not know how to apply the Word of God to be made free. As we began in 2 Corinthians, we came to the knowledge that there were specific weapons that we have been given that are for the purpose of breaking the strong holds of sin. Let us now take a look at how to cut these cords.

Obviously for the Christian, the first weapon we have is our sword, the Word of God. 2 Timothy 3:16 says, **"All scripture *is* given by inspiration of God, and *is* profitable for doctrine, for reproof, for correction, for instruction in righteousness:"** I once heard a preacher say that doctrine is what is right, reproof is what is wrong, correction is how to get it right, and instruction in righteousness is how to keep it right. We must recognize the Scripture as the sole authority for life. It is important for the Christian to cast off the world's philosophy in the battle of sin. God has given us the weapons we need. 2 Peter 1:3 says, **"According as his divine power hath given unto us all things that *pertain* unto life and godliness, through the knowledge of him that hath called us to glory and virtue:"** You may have this world's philosophy embedded in your mind, but it will not cut the cords of sin in your life. Only the Bible has the answer for that. Let us mention briefly that you must use the proper weapon. This is not a book on the defense of the King James; however, you must use the right Bible to get the right results. The King James is the right weapon to use. In our opening text of Mark 9, Jesus gave us the other two weapons that are vital to winning spiritual warfare: prayer and fasting. There are many fine books on prayer, and I believe that in this area, if you are involved in this struggle with sin, you have probably called out to God many times.

The issue of fasting is a different case. Fasting is avoided altogether by many people, and often misused by many others. Isaiah 58:3-12 is a passage that not only corrects misnomers about fasting, but also gives the specifics of proper Biblical fasting. Verse 3-7 says, "**Wherefore have we fasted,** *say they,* **and thou seest not?** *wherefore* **have we afflicted our soul, and thou takest no knowledge? Behold, in the day of your fast ye find pleasure, and exact all your labours. Behold, ye fast for strife and debate, and to smite with the fist of wickedness: ye shall not fast as** *ye do this* **day, to make your voice to be heard on high. Is it such a fast that I have chosen? a day for a man to afflict his soul?** *is it* **to bow down his head as a bulrush, and to spread sackcloth and ashes** *under him?* **wilt thou call this a fast, and an acceptable day to the LORD?** *Is* **not this the fast that I have chosen? to loose the bands of wickedness, to undo the heavy burdens, and to let the oppressed go free, and that ye break every yoke?** *Is it* **not to deal thy bread to the hungry, and that thou bring the poor that are cast out to thy house? when thou seest the naked, that thou cover him; and that thou hide not thyself from thine own flesh?"**

According to verse four, fasting is not to make your voice to be heard on high. In other words, fasting is not for the sole purpose of getting what you want. Instead, verse six tells us what purpose God had for fasting: to loose the bands of wickedness. Many times I read this as loosing the bands of the wicked as if it was talking about someone else. This verse is talking to you and me, not about other people you know. Fasting is to loose your bands of wickedness, your strongholds of sin, your cords of sin. Secondly, fasting was to undo heavy burdens. Sin in the life of a Christian becomes a very heavy burden. Thirdly, fasting helps the oppressed to go free, and fourthly, it breaks every yoke. Notice it will break EVERY yoke. When you sin you place the yoke on your neck and you begin to be a servant. As a Christian you do not have to let that yoke remain, fasting was for the purpose of breaking every yoke. Remember what Jesus said in Mark 9, "**...This kind can come forth by nothing, but by prayer and fasting.**" Fasting lets the oppressed go free. If you are in bondage to sin, fasting will break the yoke of your sin if you follow not only the proper motive, but also the proper method. Fasting is not only abstaining from food. Isaiah 58:3 told us that God did not heed the fasting because they were finding pleasure and exacting labors. Pleasure and profit are the first two things that you must abstain from when fasting. Pleasure includes eating; however, if you are diabetic you must eat. There are two schools of thought, one is to fast and trust God to keep you from dying. The other is God made you this way and expects you to not defile yourself. I believe that a diabetic should eat what is necessary to maintain their health but to abstain from indulgence. Remember the letter killeth, but the spirit giveth life. Abstaining from pleasure means you do not engage in activities of fleshly enjoyment, such as hobbies, watching TV, exercise, or anything that you do in the normal course of your day. Abstaining from profit means that you do not go to work that day, you do not do anything to profit yourself. Instead this day of fasting is spent giving yourself to prayer and the reading of God's Word.

There are two other elements to Biblical fasting found in this passage. First you should not only abstain from the pleasure of food, but you should take what you would have eaten and give it to someone in need. Dealing thy bread to the hungry is saying, I am not just putting off my pleasure, I am denying myself of it. Secondly, the scripture says in verse ten of our passage **"...draw out thy soul to the hungry, and satisfy the afflicted soul..."** This goes beyond a gift, it extends to your Biblical responsibility to minister to others.

Satan is the master of selfishness. He began introducing this philosophy to man clear back in the garden, by convincing Eve that she should be more concerned about her desires than God's commandments. Eve believed the lies of the devil. One of the biggest problem in breaking the cords of sin is identifying the lies of the devil and rejecting them for the truth of God. Even as you have been reading this booklet, you have probably had thoughts come through your mind that have cast doubt upon what the scriptures clearly say. In order to enact the truth you must reject the lies. Remember Satan is the father of lies. John 8:44 says, **"Ye are of *your* father the devil, and the lusts of your father ye will do. He was a murderer from the beginning, and abode not in the truth, because there is no truth in him. When he speaketh a lie, he speaketh of his own: for he is a liar, and the father of it."** You see, Satan is not interested in the truth; he is interested in keeping you in bondage to the sin that you have been struggling with. He has told many that they can never be free, so they might as well stop fighting and just make the best of their situation. But God told us in Corinthians that EVERY stronghold could be broken.

One of the best ways to defeat the lies of the devil is to memorize the truth. If you have been struggling with believing the truth, then you should memorize the word of God. Romans 12:2 says, **"And be not** conformed to this world: but be ye transformed by the renewing of your mind, that ye may prove what *is* that good, and acceptable, and perfect, will of God." You can follow God's word and have victory over sin.

By explaining Biblical fasting I am not promoting asceticism, which is the thought of holiness through self-affliction. I am simply saying that God has given us the principles of fasting, and that by following them, we can be delivered from the bands of wickedness. Isaiah 58:8-12 gives us a multitude of rewards that God promises to those who follow Biblical fasting. It says, "**Then shall thy light break forth as the morning, and thine health shall spring forth speedily: and thy righteousness shall go before thee; the glory of the LORD shall be thy rereward. Then shalt thou call, and the LORD shall answer; thou shalt cry, and he shall say, Here I** *am*. **If thou take away from the midst of thee the yoke, the putting forth of the finger, and speaking vanity; And** *if* **thou draw out thy soul to the hungry, and satisfy the afflicted soul; then shall thy light rise in obscurity, and thy darkness** *be* **as the noonday: And the LORD shall guide thee continually, and satisfy thy soul in drought, and make fat thy bones: and thou shalt be like a watered garden, and like a spring of water, whose waters fail not. And** *they that shall be* **of thee shall**

build the old waste places: thou shalt raise up the foundations of many generations; and thou shalt be called, The repairer of the breach, The restorer of paths to dwell in." These rewards are self explanatory. You will have light as the morning, righteousness, answered prayer, your darkness shall be as noonday, the Lord shall be your guide, He will satisfy your soul continually, your bones will be made fat, and you will be like a well-watered garden and spring that doesn't run dry. The blessings go on and on. As it is said in verse nine, you **"...take away from the midst of thee the yoke, the putting forth of the finger and the speaking vanity;"** You must take action for yourself, stop blaming others for your sin problem, and speak the truth about your sin. Now that we have examined the strongholds and the weapons, let's take a look at some specific steps.

1. Set a day aside for prayer and fasting. The Bible consistently refers to a day of fasting in Isaiah 58 and other passages. Remember on this day, you will abstain from pleasure and profit, and you will give what you would have partaken in to the hungry. This can be accomplished by taking some food or money to others you know are in need, or by giving this to your church missions program. Do not do this to be seen, and do not tell others why you are doing this. Your reward is not to be seen by men. Give this day

to nothing but fasting, Bible study, and prayer.

2. Make an inventory of all the times, places, and ways that you have participated in the particular sin that you wish to break in your life. Then confess them, claiming the blood of Jesus Christ, and asking God to cut the cord that you attached by this action. The world sometimes stumbles onto Biblical principles that work; this is one that they have stumbled across. 2 Corinthians 10:6 says, **"And having in a readiness to revenge all disobedience, when your obedience is fulfilled."** As one of their steps, Alcoholics Anonymous has members go through the process of making a fearless moral inventory of all persons you have wronged and make amends to them. It is important that you identify all areas that you have been disobedient concerning this sin, and specifically confront it before God, asking Him to cut the cord that you have attached by committing this sin. David says in Psalms 139:23-24, **"Search me, O God, and know my heart: try me, and know my thoughts: And see if *there be any* wicked way in me, and lead me into the way everlasting."** As God reveals things to you, confess them and cut the cord. This will include getting rid of the things that you used in committing your sin. You must get rid of everything that caused you to be involved. If you purchased alcohol or pornography, go to the store and make a break by telling the clerk

that you are a Christian and you need to apologize for causing them to participate in your sin. Inform them that you will no longer be purchasing these things. This is very hard, but can be a great witness. More importantly, it forcefully breaks the cords you have attached to that sin in that place.

3. Put something in the place of the sin that you have removed. Ephesians 4:22-32 says, **"That ye put off concerning the former conversation the old man, which is corrupt according to the deceitful lusts; And be renewed in the spirit of your mind; And that ye put on the new man, which after God is created in righteousness and true holiness. Wherefore putting away lying, speak every man truth with his neighbour: for we are members one of another. Be ye angry, and sin not: let not the sun go down upon your wrath: Neither give place to the devil. Let him that stole steal no more: but rather let him labour, working with *his* hands the thing which is good, that he may have to give to him that needeth. Let no corrupt communication proceed out of your mouth, but that which is good to the use of edifying, that it may minister grace unto the hearers. And grieve not the holy Spirit of God, whereby ye are sealed unto the day of redemption. Let all bitterness, and wrath, and anger, and clamour, and evil speaking, be put away from you, with all**

malice: And be ye kind one to another, tender-hearted, forgiving one another, even as God for Christ's sake hath forgiven you. As you put off the old man and his deed of sin, you must, as this passage explains, replace the deeds of sin with deeds of righteousness. If you spent a certain time in that sin, spend that time in your Bible,or in service for God in some way.

4. Keep yourself in the Word of God. If you begin to stray from a close relationship with God, the enemy will find openings to entrap you again into sin. Once you break the cords of sin in your life you must guard your heart from the attacks of Satan. Once you have cut the cords you must then guard against attaching new ones. You must guard your heart. Proverbs 4:23 says, **"Keep thy heart with all diligence; for out of it *are* the issues of life."** Romans 13:14 says, **"But put ye on the Lord Jesus Christ, and make not provision for the flesh, to *fulfil* the lusts *thereof.*"**

5. Isaiah 58:10 says, **"And *if* thou draw out thy soul to the hungry, and satisfy the afflicted soul..."** I believe as you break the cords of sin in your own life, God expects you to begin to minister to others. Many people are so self occupied that they are really of no use to the service of God. You should not be high minded thinking that you have done some great thing of yourself, but in a humble

spirit recognize that God has given you deliverance and freedom. It is your responsibility then to minister to the needs of others.

This is not just a vague idea, it is a proven Biblical formula for breaking habitual, and compulsive sins in your life. I have personally experienced God's power in breaking the bondage of sin in my life as I followed these simple Biblical principles. I trust as you follow the Bible in these things you will gain the victory you have been longing for.

CHAPTER SEVEN

My New Identity In Christ

For much of my Christian life, I struggled to understand why, if I am a new creature in Christ and old things were passed away, that I still struggled with the same old worldly desires and thoughts that I had before I trusted Christ. The preacher said, *"Walk by faith,"* but I couldn't seem to understand what that meant, or more importantly, how to accomplish it. I have found over the years that I am not alone in this conflict. As a matter of fact, multitudes of professing Christians struggle with the feeling that somehow they have missed something and there must be something wrong with them since they can't live a constantly-victorious life in Christ. In this chapter we are going to explore who we are in Christ and how to accept that new identity so that we can live the abundant life that the Bible talks about, and we desire to live.

The beginning of our understanding must come by knowing where we came from and where we are now. To understand this we must go all the way back to the beginning. Genesis 1:1 says, **"In the beginning God created the heaven and the earth."** What does that have to do with who I am? To know who you are you must first know where you have come from and what got you to the point you were. The Bible clearly teaches that God made all things. On the sixth day God made man and gave him a name. That first man was named Adam, and Genesis 1:26a it says, **"And God said, Let us make man in our image, after our likeness…"** God created man in His own image, not that we all look alike, but that we were created with three parts just like God. We were given a body, which is our physical consciousness, or how we relate to the world around us. We were given a soul, which is our self-conscious, our intellect, our will, and our emotions. The soul is how we know who we are, and relate to others. Thirdly, we were given at creation a spirit. This spirit is our God-conscious, and it is how we communicate to God, and how God communicates to us. The Bible then says in Genesis 2:7, **"And the LORD God formed man *of* the dust of the ground, and breathed into his nostrils the breath of life; and man became a living soul."** God put life into us with His own breath. Adam then, being the first man, was what you might call the head of the human race. All people are his descendents, he is your great- great- great- . . . . Grandpa.

The Bible tells us that all men were in Adam. How could that be? Well, think of your dad: if he had never have been born, then you wouldn't have been born, either. You were in your dad in that way. In the same way, your child is in you, and their children, and all those children that will come after you. Because of that, the decisions you make have an impact on successive generations. The same is true of Adam, but because he was the first man, the decision he made had an impact on the whole human race. The decision he made was to commit the sin of disobedience to God. God had told them not to eat of the fruit of a certain tree in the garden. They were free to eat of everything else, but not that one tree. Read Genesis chapter three if you are unfamiliar with the account of what Adam did. God had given a consequence to Adam, prior to his decision, and told him that if he did eat of the tree he would surely die. We know according to the Bible that Adam and Eve both ate from that tree, and they did die, not physically or in their soul, but they died spiritually. Because of that spiritual death, they had to leave the Garden of Eden. They were no longer able to fellowship with God; the part of them that had been able was dead now. In that one decision, Adam ceased having three living parts, and now only had two parts to pass on to the children that would come after him. His body and his soul were all that were left, because his spirit was dead. This is what the Bible means when it says in Romans 5:12, **"Wherefore, as by one man sin entered into the world, and death by sin; and so death passed upon all men, for that all have sinned:"** Because we were in Adam, as future children are in you, then his spiritual decision affected us all.

This is why God in His great mercy sent Jesus Christ. To give us a chance to become once again what God had intended us to be. So that we could be spiritually alive again. All men have the desire to be spiritually alive and will go to great lengths to try and feel alive, but without God who gave life to begin with it is impossible. So Jesus came to earth and took on the form of man, lived a sinless life and on the cross took our sin debt on himself. He died for our sin, just as God had decreed in the garden that the consequence of sin was death. Jesus Christ died for you, in your place, He was placed in the grave for you, and He triumphantly rose from the grave for you, to give you victory over death, hell, and the grave. This is the wonderful story of salvation: that Christ died for you. Because of Adam's sin, you were born dead, but because of Christ's sacrifice, you can be made alive again. It says in I Corinthians 15:21-22, **"For since by man *came* death, by man *came* also the resurrection of the dead. For as in Adam all die, even so in Christ shall all be made**

alive." Jesus Christ became the second and last Adam; He became the head of all those who would accept Him. Just as Adam is the head of those who are physically born, Jesus is the head of those who are Spiritually born. All men are identified with one of these two. By birth you are automatically identified with Adam, but you can by choice be identified with Christ at the time of Salvation. So then while a man is lost, he has only one point of identification; once a man is saved, he now has two. He has the old identity, who he was in Adam, and he has the new identity, who he now is in Christ.

I Corinthians 15 goes on to explain to us in verses 45-49, **"And so it is written, The first man Adam was made a living soul; the last Adam *was made* a quickening spirit. Howbeit that *was* not first which is spiritual, but that which is natural; and afterward that which is spiritual. The first man *is* of the earth, earthy: the second man *is* the Lord from heaven. As *is* the earthy, such *are* they also that are earthy: and as *is* the heavenly, such *are* they also that are heavenly. And as we have borne the image of the earthy, we shall also bear the image of the heavenly."** God's desire is for you to stop identifying with the old man, who you were in sin, and to start identifying with the new man, who you are in Christ. This is where many Christians find their difficulty, in finding their new identity.

Imagine that you are standing between two objects. On the one side of you is a dead and rotting corpse, and on the other side of you is Jesus Christ. You stand in the middle trying to decide which of these two you want to be identified with. In the past, you have always been identified with the corpse, but you didn't know it at the time. Because of your past identity you are surprisingly comfortable being identified with the corpse. Now that you are saved, you find it disgusting, and vile, yet it still has a comforting remembrance to you. The corpse represents the old nature, who you were before salvation. The Bible says in Romans 6:2 **"God forbid. How shall we, that are dead to sin, live any longer therein?"** Again in Romans 6:11, **"Likewise reckon ye also yourselves to be dead indeed unto sin, but alive unto God through Jesus Christ our Lord."** And yet again in Romans 8:10, **"And if Christ *be* in you, the body *is* dead because of sin; but the Spirit *is* life because of righteousness."** You see, God makes it clear that the old sinful nature is dead.

God gives us a great example of this in the account of Israel leaving Egypt. You remember the Children of Israel were slaves in Egypt for 400 years. They grew up identifying themselves as slaves. That is the only identity they knew. They acted like slaves, they thought like slaves, and they taught their children to act and think like slaves. But one day a man named Moses was sent from God. Moses told them that they were not intended to be slaves, and that God has something far more wonderful for them. God wanted them to be free! God had prepared a wonderful place for them, a promised land where milk and honey flowed freely. They couldn't wait, because in their hearts, they wanted to be free. God showed them His mighty power in sending ten plagues on the Egyptians, and then by the power of God they were sent out of the only land they had ever known. They followed Moses through the Red Sea, and trusted the promises of God. Because of the plagues and the destruction of Egypt, they could not go back; they were now committed. Even if they wanted to go back they could not, they were in a sense dead to Egypt.

The Children of Israel walked from the Red Sea to the Jordan River, and God told them, now that you have trusted me and come out of Egypt it is time for you to trust me with one more thing. Cross this Jordan River and allow me to run your life. The children of Israel were scared. They decided to send twelve men across the river to spy it out and see what they should expect. When the ten men got back, two of them told about the great abundance that awaited them, and how God was going to provide for them. The other ten spies told about the giants that they saw, and how hard they thought it would be to live there because of the enemies they would face. God told the Children of Israel not to worry about the giants, if you will trust Me, I will drive them away and you won't have to. Because of their unbelief, they decided not to cross over the river.

God was disappointed with their decision and because of the decision they made they spent 40 years walking around in a desert place called the wilderness of sin. It was not until all but two of the adults that had been alive at the decision not to cross the river, Joshua and Caleb, the two spies that saw what God wanted for them, had died that the Children of Israel were allowed to enter into the Promised Land at last.

The picture we see of the Children of Israel during these 40 years is exactly what we see in a person who is still standing between that rotten corpse of what they used to be and the promise of joy in Christ. Israel began to think about how good they had it back in Egypt: there were onions and garlic, they had homes and food. Yes, they were slaves, and were beaten and driven by their oppressors, but they didn't have the burden of being in this wilderness. You see, they still thought like slaves because they had never fully yielded themselves to the whole plan of God. They still thought like slaves even though they weren't slaves any longer. When a Christian is having an identity crisis, it is because he is still thinking like a slave, he is still thinking like he did when he was identified with the corpse of sin. That is why Romans 6 said to reckon yourself dead to sin. The word reckon means to count it to be so. In other words, you have to change your mind about who you are. Just like the children of Israel, if you continue to think like a slave, you will never inhabit the promises of God.

Romans 12:1-2 says, **"I beseech you therefore, brethren, by the mercies of God, that ye present your bodies a living sacrifice, holy, acceptable unto God,** *which is* **your reasonable service. And be not conformed to this world: but be ye transformed by the renewing of your mind, that ye may prove what** *is* **that good, and acceptable, and perfect, will of God."** These verses speak directly to the heart of the matter. God says that first of all that you are to present your body to God. Quit trying to decide what is acceptable to do with your body and let God determine that for you. Quit saying it is my body and I will do what I want. Instead, present your body to God as a living sacrifice, allowing God to do whatever He wants with it. God says here that to do this is only reasonable. It is not unreasonable for God to ask you to do this, just like it was not unreasonable for God to ask Israel to cross over the Jordan River. The second part of this passage deals not with the body, but the soul. It is these two areas that comprise the old man. The soul you remember is made up of the intellect, the will, and the emotions. When the Bible speaks of the mind in these verses, it is speaking not of just your thinking, but also of your will. We often say, *"I have made up my mind."* That means that my will is determined. God wants you to make one decision to follow Him, all decisions after that are only made in respect of the first to follow Christ. The problem is that many Christians have mistakenly believed that they can make a decision whether or not they want to follow Christ on each thing that comes up in life. God says we are to make only one decision: cross the river and don't go back. Your confusion comes through trying to keep one foot in the wilderness and one in the Promised Land, but you can't straddle the river of God's will in your life. If you are going to live the victorious Christian life, there must come a point that you look at that rotting corpse that is the old nature and say, *"It is time to bury you. I am not going to identify with you anymore."*

Jesus one day went to the country of the Gadareens, and as soon as He stepped off of the boat a maniac met Him. The man lived in the tombs among the dead; he cut himself and was often bound with chains to restrain him. He identified with death and when Jesus asked his name he replied, *"My name is legion for we are many,"* speaking of the demons that possessed him. He didn't tell Jesus his real name, only the identity of his sin. This is what most people do in our day. Who are you? *"I'm an alcoholic, I'm a drug addict, I'm a compulsive eater."* You see, the devil and the world want you to find your identity in your sin. They even have told you that you can never be anything else. Once an alcoholic, always an alcoholic, you know. You have been conditioned to think like a slave, and you must learn to think like the new man who is free in Christ.

God gives us another picture of what it is like when we turn back to our old ways of sinning. The Bible says in 2 Peter 2:22, **"But it is happened unto them according to the true proverb, The dog *is* turned to his own vomit again; and the sow that was washed to her wallowing in the mire."** Imagine the disgust you feel when you see a dog eating its own vomit. That is what God feels when He sees you, His child, return to your old sinful nature. We need to understand the truth that the old man is dead, and we are dead to it.

Galatians 2:20 says, **"I am crucified with Christ: nevertheless I live; yet not I, but Christ liveth in me: and the life which I now live in the flesh I live by the faith of the Son of God, who loved me, and gave himself for me."** Notice what

Paul says, "I" that is the "old I", the old man, "am crucified with Christ" The old man that was dead in trespasses and sins, was nailed to the cross in the person of Christ. "...[N]evertheless, I live..." that is the new I, the new man that is alive. Paul was saying that the old man is dead and I do not any longer identify with him, instead I now find my identity in the life of Christ. I am not what I was. I am not that dead rotting corpse of sin, and I will no longer choose to identify myself with him and his deeds.

This does not mean that I will be able to live a sinless life, but it means that I will not make sin the identifying mark in life. Instead, I will make Christ the identifying mark of my life. The secret of my new life is that it is not mine, it is Christ's life in me. Colossians 3:1-3 says, **"If ye then be risen with Christ, seek those things which are above, where Christ sitteth on the right hand of God. Set your affection on things above, not on things on the earth. For ye are dead, and your life is hid with Christ in God."** My life is not on this earth and is not in sin any longer. It is now in heaven, and in Christ. The totality of this change affects every aspect of my life. It is just as the scripture says in 2 Corinthians 5:17, **"Therefore if any man *be* in Christ, *he is* a new creature: old things are passed away; behold, all things are become new."**

So what is my new Identity? It begins when I

know that I have been changed, made new. Colossians 1:12-14 says, **"Giving thanks unto the Father, which hath made us meet to be partakers of the inheritance of the saints in light: Who hath delivered us from the power of darkness, and hath translated** *us* **into the kingdom of his dear Son: In whom we have redemption through his blood,** *even* **the forgiveness of sins:"** You see, my deliverance and transformation has already been accomplished in Christ and I am now translated into His kingdom and presence. The word translated means that God sees me differently now than He did before. Before I was an outsider, a lost man under the condemnation of sin and bound for Hell. Now my position has changed, I am now His child, an inhabitant of His kingdom, and a resident of heaven when I die.

Let's examine some of these aspects of our new Identity. I am now God's child. John 1:12 says, **"But as many as received him, to them gave he power to become the sons of God,** *even* **to them that believe on his name:"** When you accepted Christ, you became a member of a new family. You are no longer just a member of the sinful family of Adam, you are now adopted into God's family. Romans 8:15 says, **"For ye have not received the spirit of bondage again to fear; but ye have received the Spirit of adoption, whereby we cry, Abba, Father."** When you got saved, your adoption into the Family of God gave you a new Father, and a new identity. In Galatians 4:4-7, Paul explains this by saying, **"But when the fulness of the time was come, God sent forth his Son, made of a woman, made under the law, To redeem them that were under the law, that we might receive the adoption of sons. And because ye are sons, God hath sent forth the Spirit of his Son into your hearts, crying, Abba, Father. Wherefore thou art no more a servant, but a son; and if a son, then an heir of God through Christ."** As a son of God you have received the nature of your new father. 2 Peter 1:4 says, **"Whereby are given unto us exceeding great and precious promises: that by these ye might be partakers of the divine nature, having escaped the corruption that is in the world through lust."** This divine nature of our heavenly Father means that we have the ability to live this new life that we have. As His child, we are like Him. Just as a baby does not exhibit all the characteristics of his earthly father right away, neither do we exhibit all of God's Characteristics right away, but as we grow in Christ we become more and more like Him.

As His child, when we do sin, God will discipline us, just as a loving father would, but we will still be His child. He gives us an unconditional love and acceptance as His child. It says in Hebrews 12:6, **"For**

**whom the Lord loveth he chasteneth, and scour-
geth every son whom he receiveth."** The immatu-
rity of a child focuses on the discipline mentioned
here, but a more mature look at this sees the great
blessings. First, the fact of God's discipline shows
His love for us. It says whom the Lord loves, God
does not discipline us out of hate or resentment,
only out of love for us. Second, in this verse we see
that the purpose of God's discipline is to restore us
to a right relationship with Him so that we can experience the fullness of His love for us. He longs to
comfort us when we repent and turn back to Him.
We see then that my new identity begins in the fact
that I am His Child. The second aspect of this identity is also connected to this, and is that since I am
God's child, I am a joint heir with Jesus Christ of all
that is God's. I do not have to live with a "poor me"
attitude any longer, my Father is rich. All that He
possesses is now mine as I need it. He promises to
provide everything I need. Psalm 50:10 says, **"For
every beast of the forest *is* mine, *and* the cattle
upon a thousand hills."** The New Testament goes
on to say in Philippians 4:19, **"But my God shall
supply all your need according to his riches in
glory by Christ Jesus."** What a wonderful thought
to know that I am provided for by my heavenly Father. I don't need to fear, or worry. I don't need to
run back to the old ways for my provision because

I have all things in Christ. Paul said in Philippians 4:18, **"But I have all, and abound: I am full, having received of Epaphroditus the things *which were sent* from you, an odour of a sweet smell, a sacrifice acceptable, wellpleasing to God."** God used men to provide for Paul's needs, but Paul knew that it was God that was providing it.

There are many things that we could look at as part of our new identity, but here we will only look at one more, in which is found in Revelation 1:5-6. It says, **"And from Jesus Christ, *who is* the faithful witness, *and* the first begotten of the dead, and the prince of the kings of the earth. Unto him that loved us, and washed us from our sins in his own blood, And hath made us kings and priests unto God and his Father; to him *be* glory and dominion for ever and ever. Amen."** This aspect of our new identity is that God has given us a new role within His Kingdom. Before we were saved, we were only serving ourselves. We were focused on ourselves and our lives were unproductive for anything of eternal value. Now we have been given a job to perform. We have been given not just acceptance into the Kingdom of God but also a position of service in God's Kingdom. *"You are not just welcome,"* says God. *"I have made you to rule and reign with me, and to minister to me in service for me."*

One of the reasons that many people do not fully

embrace their new identity is that they have not re-
alized the great honor of the position that God has
given to them. Instead they continue to think like
the slave they were, not the king they have become
in Christ. They are torn between being a prince or
a pauper. You may say, *"If I am a king, where is my
crown? Where is my kingdom and where are my servants?"* The answer is that you are a king with Christ,
not of your own kingdom, but within His Kingdom.
It is His crown, but in Heaven, He will present you
with a crown to wear. It is His Kingdom, but He has
chosen to share with you the joy of ruling and reign-
ing with Him. We are laying up the rewards that we
will receive in Heaven with our service now. Just as
Jesus was a servant on this earth, but King of Kings
in Heaven, so, too, we are His servants while here on
earth, but in Heaven we will be the kings over which
He will rule. God has given you the opportunity to
live a life that has eternal value, not just one that has
eternal condemnation.

How then do we take on this new life? If you
remember our example from earlier, on one side of
you is a rotten stinking corpse, on the other side is
Jesus Christ. How do we bury the old man and make
our experience in life match our position in Christ?
How do we live to Christ and die to sin? The answer
to that is easier than you might think, and is found
in the concept of 2 Corinthians 5:7, "(**For we walk**

by faith, not by sight:)" The trouble with our walk to this point is that we have been trying to live the new life in the same way we lived the old life. The old life was dominated by our senses: those things that we could see, hear, smell, touch, and taste. Our new life is to be lived by faith, not by the senses of the flesh. Remember what it said in Galatians 2:20, **"I am crucified with Christ: nevertheless I live; yet not I, but Christ liveth in me: and the life which I now live in the flesh I live by the faith of the Son of God, who loved me, and gave himself for me."** You see, we are in the flesh, but we are to live by faith. This is not some mystical thing. Living by faith simply means to respond to life from God's point of view, simply taking God at His Word and acting upon it.

Someone may ask, so how about the experiences I have already had? You have probably tried to live by faith only to fall and lose hope in it. Living by faith can be likened to a young child learning to ride a bike. They start out and fall, they get bumps and bruises and may even bleed a little, but they get back on the bike and try again and again, not because they have done it before, but because they have been told that they could do it, and have seen others do it, as well. Their experience isn't what makes the difference: it is their belief. By continually acting on their belief, their experience finally matches their faith.

In his book *The Normal Christian Life*, Watchman Nee gives the following illustration: *"You probably know the illustration of Fact, Faith, and Experience walking along the top of a wall. Fact walked steadily on, turning neither to the right nor left and never looking behind. Faith followed, and all went well so long as he kept his eyes focused upon Fact; but as soon as he became concerned about Experience and turned to see how he was getting on, he lost his balance and tumbled off the wall, and poor old Experience fell down after him."*

You see, the issue of living by faith can be summed up in the idea of keeping your eyes on God's word instead of the circumstances you are under. As we face decisions in our life, faith asks, *"What does God show me to do in His Word?"* while the flesh says, *"What can I figure out?"* Proverbs 3:5-6 says, **"Trust in the LORD with all thine heart; and lean not unto thine own understanding. In all thy ways acknowledge him, and he shall direct thy paths."** The flesh wants to see and feel how to respond; Faith responds as the Bible directs even when it doesn't make sense to the flesh.

We live in a day when people operate almost exclusively on their feelings. Feelings will deceive you because feelings are usually based on our past way of thinking and training, which was according to the flesh. Your feelings are a result of your past, which was in death. You now are to operate on God's feelings. When someone offends you, you are to forgive them, even when you don't feel like it. When you do wrong, you are to repent and do right even when you don't feel like it. You see our lives are now to operate by faith, and our feelings are to be put aside. This does not mean that they go away. It means that we choose not to act on them in the same way that we did when we were identified with the old man.

The Bible illustrates this in many ways. Consider Abraham, the father of faith. He was told by God to go to a country he had never seen. He didn't even know where it was! Look what God told him in Genesis 12:1 **"Now the LORD had said unto Abram, Get thee out of thy country, and from thy kindred, and from thy father's house, unto a land that I will shew thee:"** Notice the end of this verse, **"...unto a land that I will shew thee:"** Abraham didn't receive a map, or GPS coordinates, just the instruction to go. The flesh would say, *"I can't do this,"* but faith said, *"Obey God."* The Bible says in Romans 4:3, **"For what saith the scripture? Abraham believed God, and it was counted unto him for righteousness."** We know that Abraham had no experience with this new endeavor, but he kept his eyes on the promises of God, and with faith, his experience finally matched his position with God. Walking by faith made the difference in his life.

To make our experience match our position, many times we must affirm our position instead of our feelings. Your flesh will always want to go against your spirit, and it will question the wisdom of living by faith. It is at this point that you must affirm your Biblical identity. You may pray, for instance, *"Thank you, Father, that I was crucified with you on the cross (Romans 6:6). I know it is no longer the old man who is living, but you are living in me as my very life (Galatians 2:20). I know that you are the one who has sanctified me in this matter (1 Corinthians 1:30), and I am trusting in You as my righteousness. (1 Corinthians 1:30)."*

When there is an accusation in your heart that you are still the same as you once were, you must put your spiritual eyes on the fact of the Bible and lay claim to your new identity in Christ. It will not be easy, and you will still have times of struggle and problems as you learn to walk in your new identity in Christ. But as you learn to truly walk by faith, your experience will begin to affirm that the old man is indeed dead, and that the new man is life and peace in the Lord Jesus Christ.

Many people who experience the death of a close loved one, such as a spouse or a child, have a very difficult time with the grieving process. Many of them keep things close to them that are constant reminders of their loved ones. Some keep phone messages and tape recordings that they play back over and over just to hear the voice of the departed. The Bible says when Abraham's wife Sarah died, he chose to bury her where he would not see her grave. It is normal to grieve over the death of a loved one, but to get through the grieving process, the dead must be put away from us. Many Christians cannot live a victorious life in Christ because they have never buried the old dead man out of their sight. They keep all the pictures and remembrances of their former self around to remind them. If you really want to embrace your new Identity in Christ, you need to finally bury the old man out of your sight: get rid of the keepsakes that you have protected all this time and surround yourself with life instead of death.

Don't worry about what others will say. They will not understand because they still identify with death instead of life. 1 Peter 4:1-4 says, **"Forasmuch then as Christ hath suffered for us in the flesh, arm yourselves likewise with the same mind: for he that hath suffered in the flesh hath ceased from sin; That he no longer should live the rest of** *his* **time in the flesh to the lusts of men, but to the will of God. For the time past of** *our* **life may suffice us to have wrought the will of the Gentiles, when we walked in lasciviousness, lusts, excess of wine, revellings, banquetings, and abominable idolatries: Wherein they think it strange**

that ye run not with *them* to the same excess of riot, speaking evil of *you*:" Your identity is no longer found in the sins of the past, nor is it found in the opinions of others. It is found in the life of Jesus Christ living in you. Once you begin to live in this truth, your experience will indeed match your position, and you will find your true identity in Christ, becoming the person He already sees you to be.

CHAPTER EIGHT

Dealing Biblically With Depression

Depression is a devastating and debilitating condition. It robs the child of God from any usefulness for Him and destroys his or her effectiveness in dealing with the normal trials of life.

All of us are susceptible to falling into this condition, and many great men of faith have been in this state as well. David was a man after God's own heart, yet even he was afflicted by depression at times.

The great news from the Bible is that there is a way out of depression. While it is not a place that you have to stay; it is normal to get down, but it is sin to stay there. Psalm 42 and 43 give us a look at depression and the pathway out of it. Notice the darkness of depression as you read through these passages now.

Psalm 42:1-11 **"As the hart panteth after the water brooks, so panteth my soul after thee, O God. My soul thirsteth for God, for the living God: when shall I come and appear before God? My tears have been my meat day and night, while** they continually say unto me, Where *is* thy God? When I remember these *things*, I pour out my soul in me: for I had gone with the multitude, I went with them to the house of God, with the voice of joy and praise, with a multitude that kept holyday. Why art thou cast down, O my soul? and *why* art thou disquieted in me? hope thou in God: for I shall yet praise him *for* the help of his countenance. O my God, my soul is cast down within me: therefore will I remember thee from the land of Jordan, and of the Hermonites, from the hill Mizar. Deep calleth unto deep at the noise of thy waterspouts: all thy waves and thy billows are gone over me. *Yet* the LORD will command his lovingkindness in the daytime, and in the night his song *shall be* with me, *and* my prayer unto the God of my life. I will say unto God my rock, Why hast thou forgotten me? why go I mourning because of the oppression of the enemy? As with a sword in my bones, mine enemies reproach me; while they say daily unto me, Where *is* thy God? Why art thou cast down, O my soul? and why art thou disquieted within me? hope thou in God: for I shall yet praise him, *who is* the health of my countenance, and my God."

Psalm 43:1-5 **"Judge me, O God, and plead my cause against an ungodly nation: O deliver me**

from the deceitful and unjust man. For thou *art* the God of my strength: why dost thou cast me off? why go I mourning because of the oppression of the enemy? O send out thy light and thy truth: let them lead me; let them bring me unto thy holy hill, and to thy tabernacles. Then will I go unto the altar of God, unto God my exceeding joy: yea, upon the harp will I praise thee, O God my God. Why art thou cast down, O my soul? and why art thou disquieted within me? hope in God: for I shall yet praise him, *who is* the health of my countenance, and my God."

David here uses some very dark metaphors and even some direct statements to express the depression that he is in. Take a special look at verse 9 where he tells us the source of the problem. It says that he goes mourning because of the oppression of the enemy. He doesn't say my enemy, or thy enemy, or an enemy, he says the enemy.

While this might be emblematic of saying he was talking about his personal enemy, God doesn't mix words. Jesus used the same phrase to refer to the Devil in Matthew 13:39 when He said, **"The enemy that sowed them is the devil; the harvest is the end of the world; and the reapers are the angels."** And again in Luke 10:19 where it says, **"Behold, I give unto you power to tread on serpents and scorpions, and over all the power of the enemy:**

and nothing shall by any means hurt you."

Depression is not God's plan for you! God's plan is peace that passes understanding, He has not given us a spirit of fear, but of power, of love and of a sound mind. Notice that David sees the opposite of his state in verse 5 and verse 11 as he says, **"Why art thou cast down, O my soul? and *why* art thou disquieted in me?..."** Hope in God! David then defines Hope as the opposite of Depression. A depressed person is a person without hope.

David further indicates that the only place to get help is from the Lord. Notice in verse 5 he says he will praise him for the help of His countenance. Then in verse 11 David says that God is the health of my countenance. In other words, the health of my countenance is found in the help of His countenance. Drugs are not the answer for depression, they only mask the problem; they treat the symptom not the source. Drugs don't give hope back to the soul; they only trick the brain.

David knew that His only hope to escape depression was to get close to God, so that is why He started off the Psalm like he did, **"As the hart panteth after the water brooks, so panteth my soul after thee, O God. My soul thirsteth for God, for the living God: when shall I come and appear before God?"**

Now let's take note that this is David, the mighty

King of Israel, the conqueror of all that he goes to battle with, the man after God's own heart. Many times when we find ourselves in depression we think that we are the only ones who ever felt this way, and there must be something very wrong with us because we are like this, but even David found himself in this state.

So to find yourself in depression is not abnormal, but it is a sign that you are in a spiritual battle. It could be that your depression is because you haven't recognized that battle as such and turned to God for help, or it could be that you have given Satan access to oppress you because of sin. Remember, whatsoever is not of faith is sin. To be without hope is really to be dwelling in a sinful state. While you might find yourself there, a child of God should not stay there.

David knows that it is not God's will for a person to stay in depression. But he also is searching his soul to determine where he has fallen into this oppression of the enemy, notice how many times he asks why? A depressed person will often ask themselves why do I feel this way, why, why, why. The answer is that you allowed your thinking to be co-opted by the oppression of the enemy. As a man thinketh in his heart so is he. What you think will determine how you feel, and how you feel will determine how you act.

The key to overcoming depression is to identify where your thinking isn't right; where did I believe Satan's lie and deviate my thinking from God's word? Once you have identified the error, then you must change your thinking. David gives us five answers on how to do this in this passage.

The first step is to begin to Praise God. Isaiah 61:3 tells us, **"To appoint unto them that mourn in Zion, to give unto them beauty for ashes, the oil of joy for mourning, the garment of praise for the spirit of heaviness; that they might be called trees of righteousness, the planting of the LORD, that he might be glorified."**

Praise is literally the opposite of depression; the word depression means to sink down or to be pushed downward, while praise means to lift up and to exalt. The irony is that lifting God up requires the act of humbling ourselves as well. Depression is the feeling that we are low; humility is through the feeling that He is high. Though you might say these things are similar, the latter comes with a great promise, James 4:10 says, **"Humble yourselves in the sight of the Lord, and he shall lift you up."**

Truly the first step to recovery from depression is to go lower, in humility. It is not infrequent to find someone who is battling with depression who is also a very prideful person. In reality they are depressed because they think that they deserve better than what they have received. It is actually their act of lifting themselves up that has caused them to be pushed down. If they would humble themselves instead and lift Him up, they would be lifted up themselves. I am not saying that everyone who gets depressed does so because of pride; I am saying that humility is necessary for proper praise.

We teach people how to do this in Biblical counseling by having them do a stroke file. They take a 3x5 card and on the front of it they will write three things in the morning, three things at noon, and three things in the evening that they can thank God for. David prayed three times a day in this manner. Psalm 55:17 says, **"Evening, and morning, and at noon, will I pray, and cry aloud: and he shall hear my voice."** Daniel prayed three times a day, according to the book of Daniel. As a matter of fact, he was so faithful in this that this is how his enemies attacked him.

Three times a day you should take time to seek the Lord and praise Him. This will keep His glory before your eyes all day long. If you are struggling with depression, you should begin to keep a stroke file today. On the back we teach people to write the name of their spouse, and once each morning, noon, and night write one thing that they can be thankful for about them. It could be things that they do, or it could be things they don't do. If your spouse isn't strung out on drugs, that is a great reason to thank

God.

The next step that David takes is to remember God. This means to look back on your life and purposely remember all the things that God has done for you. When we are depressed we only see the negative and bad things. It would be a good idea to get a notebook and begin to write down all the good things you can remember that God did for you. Philippians 4:8 says, **"Finally, brethren, whatsoever things are true, whatsoever things *are* honest, whatsoever things *are* just, whatsoever things *are* pure, whatsoever things *are* lovely, whatsoever things *are* of good report; if *there be* any virtue, and if *there be* any praise, think on these things."**

Notice in Psalm 42:6 that David had some special places of remembrance to God. He considered the land of Jordan; this was the promised land, that place of the promises of God. Remember the works of God as He brought His people across the Jordan River and began to give them the place of their inheritance. As David looked around, it was a reminder of the fulfillment of the promises of God everywhere that he looked. Maybe there is a special place in your life where you received the promises of God. Consider that place and what God did there for you.

Then David remembered the Hermonites. Psalm 133:3 says, **"As the dew of Hermon, *and as the dew***

that descended upon the mountains of Zion: for there the LORD commanded the blessing, *even* **life for evermore."** The Hermonites are the mountain range on the north border of Israel. The Hermonites were a place where David had received the commandment of blessing from the Lord.

Is there a time in your life that you remember God speaking to you? You should remember that time of God's speaking, and think on the times that God has spoken in your life. David further remembers the hill Mizar, which is a peak in the mountain range. It is not clear exactly what happened here, but this was a special place for David, and as he recalled what he experienced in this place, it is clear that he remembered the blessing that God gave him there.

There are some times of blessing in your life that, if you will keep them in remembrance, it will bring you up out of depression. There are some mountaintop experiences that God has given each of us that will strengthen our hearts.

The next thing we see David do is to seek his commandments in the day. Consider the following Scriptures. Psalm 119:50 **"This** *is* **my comfort in my affliction: for thy word hath quickened me."** Psalm 119:81 **"My soul fainteth for thy salvation:** *but* **I hope in thy word."** Psalm 119:114 **"Thou** *art* **my hiding place and my shield: I hope in thy word."** David delighted himself in God's Word and there he found strength and encouragement. Psalm 119:130 tells us, **"The entrance of thy words giveth light; it giveth understanding unto the simple."** Notice what David did when he had come to a place of depression in 1 Samuel 30:6, **"And David was greatly distressed; for the people spake of stoning him, because the soul of all the people was grieved, every man for his sons and for his daughters: but David encouraged himself in the LORD his God."** Romans 10:17 tells us, **"So then faith *cometh* by hearing, and hearing by the word of God."** To strengthen your faith you need to listen to the Word. You can get a copy of the Bible and keep it in your home, and it will strengthen you. It will do a lot more for you than Ellen or Oprah, I guarantee.

When in times of depression read the Psalms; they are encouragement to the soul.

David goes on from this and says that to recover from depression you should sing songs in the night. All through the Bible we see a strong connection between the spirit and music. Saul, when he was troubled by an evil spirit, had David play on the harp and sang, and the evil spirit would depart. Samuel, when seeking the Lord, had them play music. David was the sweet Psalmist of Israel; Solomon also wrote Psalms and had a great choir that sang at the temple. Music is an expression of the soul, thus it not only brings sorrow, but joy. Someone who is struggling with depression should surround themselves with Godly, uplifting music.

The last of the five steps that David took was to spend time in prayer. Philippians 4:6-7 says, **"Be careful for nothing; but in every thing by prayer and supplication with thanksgiving let your requests be made known unto God. And the peace of God, which passeth all understanding, shall keep your hearts and minds through Christ Jesus."** When in a state of depression many times the last thing that we want to do is pray, when in reality it should be the first thing that we do.

Revelation 12:11 tells us, **"And they overcame him by the blood of the Lamb, and by the word of their testimony; and they loved not their lives unto the death."** To plead the blood, and speak of the testimony of what God has done for us is how we see the enemy being defeated over and over again in the Bible.

This is the place that we find David at the beginning of Psalm 43; He is praying. In Psalm 42 David deals primarily with what the depressed should do, but in Psalm 43 we find out what God does in response to our obedience in these five things. Psalm 43 begins with an honest prayer for God to examine Him. He says, **"Judge me, O God, and plead my cause against an ungodly nation: O deliver me**

from the deceitful and unjust man. For thou *art* the God of my strength: why dost thou cast me off? why go I mourning because of the oppression of the enemy? O send out thy light and thy truth: let them lead me; let them bring me unto thy holy hill, and to thy tabernacles." The word judge here is not a cry for condemnation, but for examination and help. It is the thought of one who might inspect an item that is imperfect so that it might be corrected.

The last thing that a person who is in depression wants is judgment, but it is the thing that they need, not the judgment of people, but the honest examination of God in their lives. This is accomplished by two means in this passage.

The first way that God examines us is by His light. Light began with God when He said, let there be light and there was light; that is physically. However, the light that is spiritual began with Him as well, and it is by Him speaking the light into our darkened hearts that we are illuminated. The darkness of depression is a place without the light of God illuminating it, thus He must speak His light into such a place.

That doesn't mean that a person who is in depression isn't in the Word, but that God must illuminate His Word in them, the power of the Word of God is His Holy Spirit illumination of it. Consider the following verses, Psalm 4:6 "*There be* **many that say, Who will shew us** *any* **good? LORD, lift thou up the light of thy countenance upon us.**" Psalm 36:9 "**For with thee** *is* **the fountain of life: in thy light shall we see light.**"

And Psalm 97:11 "**Light is sown for the righteous, and gladness for the upright in heart.**" Wow! I like that verse. Consider the thought here: Light is sown. We think in terms of sowing a seed, but God sows light, meaning it is planted for a purpose; it is not just floating around aimlessly. Physical light is sown by God for the purpose of bringing forth the fruit of the ground thus making provision for us.

Spiritual light has been sown as well; it was sown by Jesus Christ in His death, burial and resurrection. It was also sown in His Word, and it in such a manner has been planted for the purpose of bringing forth more light. Much fruit is produced by the planting of one seed, so too much light is produced by the sowing of light. Psalm 112:4 says, "**Unto the upright there ariseth light in the darkness:** *he is* **gracious, and full of compassion, and righteous.**" Psalm 119:105 says, "**Thy word** *is* **a lamp unto my feet, and a light unto my path.**" And Psalm 119:130 tells us, "**The entrance of thy words giveth light; it giveth understanding unto the simple.**"

God's response to our obedience is to begin to

shed His light into the darkness of our depression and illuminate our souls.

The next thing that God uses to judge us is His truth. Psalm 119:151 says, **"Thou *art* near, O LORD; and all thy commandments *are* truth."** Jesus said in John 17:17 **"Sanctify them through thy truth: thy word is truth."** When God's Word is sent out to our hearts, it reveals what is in error in our hearts. We said before that the reason for depression is that we have believed a lie from the enemy. Only the acceptance of the truth can challenge the lie and correct it.

Once we accept that God's Word is truth, and begin to ask Him to judge us and correct our error by it, we must commit ourselves to obey whatever He tells us to do. James 1:22-25 says, **"But be ye doers of the word, and not hearers only, deceiving your own selves. For if any be a hearer of the word, and not a doer, he is like unto a man beholding his natural face in a glass: For he beholdeth himself, and goeth his way, and straightway forgetteth what manner of man he was. But whoso looketh into the perfect law of liberty, and continueth *therein*, he being not a forgetful hearer, but a doer of the work, this man shall be blessed in his deed."**

The result of yielding ourselves to the examination of God's light and truth is shown to produce results in Psalm 43. Here we find out that they lead us. Part of the struggle of addiction is that there is no clear direction for life that is known. Likewise a depressed person is wandering aimlessly. Life has no meaning or purpose, but God's Word gives a leading a purpose when it is applied to our lives.

David goes on to show where God's Word leads us: first to God's holy hills, then to God's tabernacles, and then to His alter. There is a natural progression of restoration that is presented here. First he comes to the holy hills, that is the city of Zion; then he comes to the tabernacles, that is the place of God's presence; and then to the alter, that is the place of my acknowledgment of God.

In everything there is a progression of accomplishing the goal. The goal in Psalm 42 was close fellowship, here God reveals that in order to have that close fellowship you first have to get in the right proximity of God's will and reject the lies of the enemy. Then you must come to the place of worshiping Him as He should be worshiped.

Once you have been brought to this place, you will find what you have been searching for all along. As David says in the last verse of Psalm 43, **"Why art thou cast down, O my soul? and why art thou disquieted within me? hope in God: for I shall yet praise him, *who is* the health of my countenance, and my God."**

There is health for your countenance, and hope for your soul in God if you will obey Him and allow Him to search you and accept His truth.

CHAPTER NINE

Overcoming Anger

From the time that I was a young person I dealt with anger in a sinful way. When something would happen that made me mad, I would blow up. I would get red faced and yell, I would even hit the wall to take my frustration out, not the most safe, nor productive, way to deal with anger. When I got married I carried my wrong response to anger into my marriage relationship. My wife when she would get angry would clam up, she wouldn't say a word. Me, on the other hand, I would shout and scream. The whole neighborhood would know that I was angry. Over time my wife began to respond to anger in the same way that I did, and we would have some humdinger fights. Praise the Lord they never got physical, but the angry words that we would say to each other would cut and wound worse than any punch ever could. After a few years of sinful response to anger our marriage was in a precarious place. Though I was pastoring at the time, the Lord saw fit to move us to go to school at Beth Haven Biblical Counselors Seminary in Oklahoma City, and begin to study Biblical counseling. It was there that God began to teach me how to get a hold of my spirit and control my anger.

Anger has become one of the biggest problems facing families today. Anger is defined in the Webster's 1828 dictionary as *"a violent passion of the mind excited by a real or supposed injury usually accompanied with a propensity to take vengeance, or to obtain satisfaction from the offending party."* The level that anger has approached in our day is alarming and revealed in the following statistics.

According to SafeYouth.com more than 1 in 3 high school students, both male and female, have been involved in a physical fight. 1 in 9 of those students have been injured badly enough to need medical treatment.

According to the Sunday Times Magazine of London England on July 16, 2006, 45% of us regularly lose our temper at work.

More than 80% of drivers say they have been involved in road rage incidents, 25% have committed an act of road rage themselves.

50% of us have reacted to computer problems by hitting our PC, hurling parts of it around, screaming or abusing our colleagues.

68% said driving to work in rush hour increases anxieties.

85% had become angry at office machinery that was not working.

Anger closely associated with stress is a major problem; up to 60% of all absences from work are caused by stress.

Stress is now bigger than the common cold as the main reason for time off.

36% of the US work force claims to come home totally exhausted from work.

The University of North Carolina found that those with a short fuse are more likely to smoke and drink, and are 2.7 times more likely to have a heart attack than someone of a calmer disposition. Stress hormones could cause an increase risk of heart disease by constricting blood vessels and causing blood clots, which could block the heart.

The University of Michigan found that men who bottle up emotions until they lose their tempers in violent outbursts are twice as likely to suffer a stroke than men with a calmer disposition. Young women who express their anger and aggression frequently have higher cholesterol levels than more placid women.

All of this demonstrates to us what we already know: anger is a serious problem. You know it personally, you have experienced the effects of anger in your own life and know how devastating it is. The first question that we want to address is, where does anger come from. We live in a society that likes to play the blame game. We would like to blame others, and probably have, for our angry outbursts. Listen to what Jesus had to say in Mark 7:14-23, **"And when he had called all the people *unto him*, he said unto them, Hearken unto me every one *of you*, and understand: There is nothing from without a man, that entering into him can defile him: but the things which come out of him, those are they that defile the man. If any man have ears to hear, let him hear. And when he was entered into the house from the people, his disciples asked him concerning the parable. And he saith unto them, Are ye so without understanding also? Do ye not perceive, that whatsoever thing from without entereth into the man, *it* cannot defile him; Because it entereth not into his heart, but into the belly, and goeth out into the draught, purging all meats? And he said, That which cometh out of the man, that defileth the man. For from within, out of the heart of men, proceed evil thoughts, adulteries, fornications, murders, Thefts, covetousness, wickedness, deceit, lasciviousness, an evil eye, blasphemy, pride, foolishness: All these evil things come from within, and defile the man."**

It is important that you understand that anger is not something that comes from outside and works its way into your heart and mind, it is something that is inside to begin with; outside circumstances and people only bring out what is already there. Anger is much like character: pressure does not create it, but rather reveals what is actually there.

Before we go further, let's understand that anger is an emotion, and all emotions are given by God and serve a purpose. We find in the Bible that God experiences these emotions just as we do, but the difference is that God never sins through these emotions. By God's example we learn the right way to deal with anger. God deals with all things in a righteous manner, thus God is angry and sins not. Not only does God not respond in a sinful manner, but God is also described in the Bible as having righteous anger. In other words, He is not selfishly motivated, it is anger because of harm coming to those whom He loves. These harms were caused by either those who were the enemies of His people or by sin that they had yielded themselves to that brought destruction to them. Thus God's anger was never selfish, and He never responded sinfully.

The problem we are really talking about is the wrong use of anger, the wrong expression of anger. Paul says in Ephesians 4:26 **"Be ye angry, and sin not: let not the sun go down upon your wrath:"** Biblically we can learn where anger comes from by examining several principles. You just read in Mark

7 about the principle that says that sinful respons-
es come from our heart. Jeremiah 17:9 says, **"The
heart *is* deceitful above all *things*, and desperate-
ly wicked: who can know it?"** Anger itself isn't the
real problem in your heart. The problems are, *"Why
do I get angry?"* and, *"What do I do about it?"* If I am
to stem the tide of sinful anger, I must stop blaming
everyone around me and take responsibility for the
fact that it is my own heart problem that is causing
this trouble. Sin has destroyed your heart and your
thinking. You must come to the place that you admit
that your sin has brought destruction into your life.

The sinful response to anger is as much sin as
murder. As a matter of fact, God likens it to be the
same thing in Matthew 5:21-22, **"Ye have heard
that it was said by them of old time, Thou shalt
not kill; and whosoever shall kill shall be in danger of the judgment: But I say unto you, That
whosoever is angry with his brother without a
cause shall be in danger of the judgment: and
whosoever shall say to his brother, Raca, shall
be in danger of the council: but whosoever shall
say, Thou fool, shall be in danger of hell fire."** You
may say that this doesn't apply to you because you
always have a cause to be angry. The problem is that
your causes always seem to center around what others have done; you are trapped in the cycle of responding to life rather than preparing biblically for

it. The answer is not to change what is outside, and adjust your circumstances; the answer is to change that which is inside your heart, and only Jesus can do that. Ezekiel 36:26 says, **"A new heart also will I give you, and a new spirit will I put within you: and I will take away the stony heart out of your flesh, and I will give you an heart of flesh."** And 2 Corinthians 5:17 tells us, **"Therefore if any man *be* in Christ, *he is* a new creature: old things are passed away; behold, all things are become new."** This is the principle of the new creation, that in Christ we are forgiven, and we are made new. We are given a new life. I cannot do it on my own, but in Him I can do all things.

Dealing with anger biblically begins when we recognize that it is a heart problem. The Bible teaches us in Proverbs 23:7 **"For as he thinketh in his heart, so *is* he: Eat and drink, saith he to thee; but his heart *is* not with thee."** The heart of the matter is how you have been thinking about things. And the first area to start to change your thinking in is your expectations. Psalm 62:5 says, **"My soul, wait thou only upon God; for my expectation *is* from him."** This is a little verse, but it packs a mighty thought. Most anger is the result of broken expectations. You expected someone to do a certain thing, or act a certain way and they disappointed you so you got angry. You expected something to happen in a certain time and it didn't so you got angry. David teaches here in Psalm 62:5 that you should not have your expectations set on anyone or anything other than what God has told you to. Jeremiah 17:5 tells us, **"Thus saith the LORD; Cursed *be* the man that trusteth in man, and maketh flesh his arm, and whose heart departeth from the LORD."** When you put your trust in men, you put yourself under a curse, the curse is that they will fail you, they will break your expectations and you will be disappointed. As a matter of fact you can't even put expectations in yourself because Jeremiah 10:23 says, **"O LORD, I know that the way of man *is* not in himself: *it is* not in man that walketh to direct his steps."** God didn't make you with the ability to direct your own steps. You don't know if you have another breath but by the grace of God, so how can you trust in yourself.

Sinful anger is the result of the curse of unbiblical expectations, and left unchecked it will lead to bitterness, resentment, vengeance, ingratitude, and depression. You may feel that you have a right to be angry, but what you really have is an unbiblical thinking process. It may be that God keeps allowing your goals and plans to be blocked because He wants you to stop trying to run your own life and turn it over to Him. The answer isn't just to put your expectations in other plans or people; a change of scenery won't change the problem of your heart. The answer is to get Biblical expectations. You see, David didn't tell us that his expectation was in God, but rather that it was from God. Some people are angry at God because they had an expectation of him, but not from Him. They expected that He would do things their way but He has a better way. God is not bound to meet your expectations; He does not have to. You are the one that should get your expectations from Him rather than demanding Him to measure up to your plans. To receive an expectation from His means that you see in His Word a promise and you claim it. God always keeps His Word. Romans 10:13 says, **"For whosoever shall call upon the name of the Lord shall be saved."** You can have a biblical expectation that if you call upon Jesus Christ to be your Lord and Saviour, you are saved. That is receiving an expectation from Him. Philippians 4:19 tells us, **"But my God shall supply all your need according to his riches in glory by Christ Jesus."** You can have an expectation from God that He will provide for you if you are His child. You see an expectation from God is one that His Word has told you to have.

Once we have dealt with the source and identified that sinful anger comes from our hearts when we have set wrong expectations, we must then deal with the fact that our response to anger has been wrong, as well. There are two primary ways that people deal with anger in a sinful way. The first wrong response is to take it out on themselves and internalize it. The anger builds up and builds up in them until it has no outlet and they start the downward spiral of destruction into bitterness and depression. People who deal with anger in this way self destruct, their stress level is always high, and their body begins to destroy itself because of it. It manifests itself in multitudes of emotional and physical problems. They may or may not be hurting other people, but their sinful response to anger is killing them. The other sinful way that people deal with anger is to take it out on others. These people blow up and attack those around them. A lady once came to Billy Sunday and tried to rationalize her angry outbursts. *"There's nothing wrong with losing my temper,"* she said. *"I blow up, and then it's all over." "So does a shotgun,"* Sunday replied, *"and look at the damage it leaves behind!"* People who respond to anger in this way are destroyers: they destroy relationships, marriages, and families. They hack and chop at others with their anger until they wound and alienate everyone in their life. Some people who respond this way to anger may not have many health problems, but most will have high tension rates and other emotional and physical problems over time that hurt them as well.

One of the biggest problems with the sinful response to anger is that it is perpetuated from generation to generation. Proverbs 22:5 says, **"Train up a child in the way he should go: and when he is old, he will not depart from it."** If you deal with anger sinfully, you are also teaching your children to deal with anger sinfully. For years I did counseling with children and parents would bring their child in and say, *"They just cannot control their anger."* The whole time the parents were trying to maintain that they didn't have any problems with anger, but where do you suppose the child learned to respond that way? Of course, they learned their response from the parents. The parent's didn't respond to anger in the right way and the child took it to the next level. You may look back on your childhood and see that your parents responded wrong to anger, as well. That is not an excuse to act out yourself; you still have a choice. You can choose to begin responding to anger with a biblical approach and salvage your family from the clutches of this generational sin.

Let's begin now to take a look at how to respond biblically to anger. There are three things that we must do in responding the right way to anger. First, we must examine ourselves and recognize the wrong thinking in our heart that produced the anger. What expectation did I have that was broken, and why did I set my expectation there instead of in God's Word?

I cannot continue to blame others when I get angry; I must take the responsibility for it. As soon as you get angry, stop and pray, ask the Lord to help you see the false expectation that you had so that you can fix it and have a biblical expectation instead. Always remember that you don't have to respond sinfully: that is a choice. Satan will lie to you and say that you cannot help it, that is just how you are. But you can help it, and you do have a choice! You can do as it says in 2 Corinthians 10:5 **"Casting down imaginations, and every high thing that exalteth itself against the knowledge of God, and bringing into captivity every thought to the obedience of Christ;"** You are not a victim; you are an overcomer through Christ Jesus and you have His Spirit living within you so that you do not have to yield yourself to sin. Take those sinful thoughts captive, cast them out, and choose to walk in obedience to Christ.

The next step that you must take once you have identified the wrong expectation is to attack the problem. If the problem involves someone else, the person is not the problem, but why they did or did not do what they should. One way you can effectively approach someone without confrontation is to speak to them with "I" messages. For example, you may say to them, *"I have a problem that I need your help with."* The truth is that if you are the one getting angry, you are the one with the problem. Approaching someone using an "I" message diffuses their feeling of being attacked and eases the situation. You can then begin to explain your side of the situation while asking for their help to rectify the problem. As you begin to deal with problems in this manner you should take time to pray and ask the Lord to give you wisdom and calmness to approach the situations in a godly and biblical manner.

As you grow in the Lord you should begin to look at problems and trials as opportunities to see the Lord work in your life. The ultimate goal in the Christian life is to walk in the Spirit. Galatians 5:16 says, **"*This* I say then, Walk in the Spirit, and ye shall not fulfil the lust of the flesh."** When we respond to anger in a sinful way, we are declaring that we are walking in the flesh. To say that I cannot deal with anger in a biblical way is to reveal that I am not spiritual enough to respond properly.

When you choose to walk in the Spirit and attack the problem in a biblical way instead of yielding to your flesh, you are going to see God begin to bless your life and your relationships again. This brings us to the last step in dealing with anger in a biblical way: choosing biblical forgiveness. It may be that your anger is a result of building up conflicts in your life that are yet unresolved. The only way to deal with this is to learn about God's way of forgiveness.

Forgiveness is something that is very important to God, as a matter of fact it is so important that God says in Matthew 6:15, **"But if ye forgive not men their trespasses, neither will your Father forgive your trespasses."** God will withhold forgiveness from you if you refuse to forgive others.

People usually try to forgive in one of two ways, either with emotional or logical forgiveness. Emotional forgiveness says, *"I don't feel like being angry any longer, and so I will forgive."* I may not feel like fighting, or just want to have a moment of peace, so I will say "I forgive" based on how I feel. The problem with this type of forgiveness is that feelings change. That is why someone can forgive, and then bring it up the next time they fight. Now they don't feel like forgiving for that any longer. Logical forgiveness says, *"I think that it makes sense to forgive."* I think that it makes sense because I don't like the consequences of not forgiving, or I think something else is more important. Logical forgiveness also doesn't work because it continues to keep score; eventually it won't make sense any longer.

The only type of forgiveness that truly works is spiritual forgiveness. This type of forgiveness is based on the example of Christ and is illustrated in 2 Corinthians 2:10-11 by Paul when He says, **"To whom ye forgive any thing, I *forgive* also: for if I forgave any thing, to whom I forgave *it*, for your**

sakes *forgave I it* in the person of Christ; Lest
Satan should get an advantage of us: for we are
not ignorant of his devices." Paul is saying that he
forgives in the person of Christ. In other words, he
considers Christ when He was on the cross, and on
the cross all the sins of all men were placed on Him.
Jesus took all those sins and chose to pay for them
regardless of how He felt or what He thought. That
means that the offence that was committed against
you was placed upon Jesus on the cross and there
He chose to die to forgive it. True forgiveness is just
that. It is choosing Jesus over your feelings and your
thoughts. It is saying that if Jesus Christ could die
to forgive that sin, I can choose to accept that He
knows more than I do and He always chooses the
right way, so I will choose to operate based on His
decisions rather than my own. This spiritual forgiveness is a daily choice: to choose to die with Christ
to our thinking and feelings is necessary. Paul said in
Galatians 2:20, "I am crucified with Christ: nevertheless I live; yet not I, but Christ liveth in me:
and the life which I now live in the flesh I live by
the faith of the Son of God, who loved me, and
gave himself for me." And then in 1 Corinthians
15:31, "I protest by your rejoicing which I have
in Christ Jesus our Lord, I die daily." Daily I must
remember that if I am saved my old life was crucified with Christ on the cross and I must choose to

walk each day in that death to self.

You see the truth is that the person that offended you doesn't deserve forgiveness, but neither did you, and Jesus forgave you anyway. Jesus was very pointed in His description of forgiveness when He said in Matthew 6:15, **"But if ye forgive not men their trespasses, neither will your Father forgive your trespasses."** What right do you have to ask God to forgive your sins, if you will not forgive others their sins. If we all got what we deserved we would be cast into hell, but thanks be to God that by Jesus Christ we receive mercy and not justice. Spiritual forgiveness is choosing God over your thinking and feelings. When you do that, you stop the downward spiral of anger and you keep Satan from getting the advantage over you. When you acknowledge just how much Jesus forgave you for, you will love Him more. The Bible tells us in 1 Peter 4:8, **"And above all things have fervent charity among yourselves: for charity shall cover the multitude of sins."** Love God and you will love others, love others and you will lose your anger.

This is the truth that God showed me after years of responding in anger: the real problem that I had was that I didn't love Jesus enough to respond as He would respond. By my angry response to adversity I was declaring that I was not spiritual enough to respond properly, and the only reason for a believer not being spiritual enough is a lack of love for the Lord. I made a decision that I would choose to walk in the Spirit instead of the flesh. The day the Lord showed me the truth about myself and my anger I went home I told my wife what God had shown me and apologized for my sinful response to anger. It took a while for her to begin to reflect my new decision back to me. I had trained her for many years to respond sinfully, as well. The thing that God had to teach me was that it doesn't matter how other people respond, if I will allow Him to set my expectations, and walk in the Spirit, forgiving and loving, no one can make me angry, I am in control of my own spirit and it is my responsibility to govern it by the Word of God. You, too, can respond properly. You do not have to be a slave to your anger, you can have a life free from the power of this sin if you will apply the Word of God that you have learned here.

CHAPTER TEN

Sin's Effects

Nothing affects man more than sin. Sin devastates every aspect of man, and is complete in its destruction of the body and soul. The curious thing about sin is that every person believes that they are the one that will not be destroyed by it. That somehow they will be able to escape the inevitable consequences of sin and be unscathed. We know that this is an impossible hope. James 1:15 says, **"Then when lust hath conceived, it bringeth forth sin: and sin, when it is finished, bringeth forth death."** God by his goodness has endeavored to reveal to man the eternal consequences of sin, spending eternity in the lake of fire separated from him, by allowing man to suffer the painful affects of sin in this life. Galatians 6:7-8 tells us, **"Be not deceived; God is not mocked: for whatsoever a man soweth, that shall he also reap. For he that soweth to his flesh shall of the flesh reap corruption; but he that soweth to the Spirit shall of the Spirit reap life everlasting."**

As a young man living in my parents home my father did some dry land wheat farming on land that my grandmother had inherited in western Kansas. Each year he and I would go to the land and prepare it for planting the wheat, then in fall we would plant. The next spring we would come back to find a beautiful field of green coming up. In June or early July the wheat would be gold and ready to harvest. In all the time that we spent farming we never came back in the spring and found water melons. We never found peach trees, corn, or any other form of vegetation, we always found wheat. The reason seems very obvious, the reason we always found wheat is because that is what we always planted. So it is with sin. Many people plant sin in their lives and plow iniquity and wickedness all the while thinking that they will never have a crop come in. They are mistaken, God will not be mocked and a man will reap the effects of the sin that he sows in his life.

Psalms 38 is a portion of scripture that was written by David, as he cried out to God in anguish over the effects sin had in his life. The Bible calls David a man after God's own heart, we see David as a man who God blessed greatly. None was as favored by God as David was during his life, and we would say that very few men have ever given themselves to God and loved God as much as David did. However, we see in the scripture that David was not immune to the effects of sin. This passage was likely written after David had sinned with Bathsheeba. Many times we consider this to be just a terrible act of adultery, but in this account we see that Broke nearly all of the ten commandments. He coveted his neighbor's wife, stole his neighbor's wife, committed adultery, committed murder, lied about his sin, dishonored his parents, dishonored God, and by doing so blasphemed the name of God, David placed his own selfish lust up as an idol in place of God. Which man, however, could honestly say that they are not guilty of breaking God's law as well. Romans 3:10-12 tells us **"As it is written, There is none righteous, no, not one: There is none that understandeth, there is none that seeketh after God. They are all gone out of the way, they are together become unprofitable; there is none that doeth good, no, not one. They are all gone out of the way, they are together become unprofitable; there is none that doeth good, no, not one."**

What God Does When We Sin

David begins his explanation of what sin had done to him by sharing what God did when he sinned. Psalms 38:1-2 says, **"O LORD, rebuke me not in thy wrath: neither chasten me in thy hot displeasure. For thine arrows stick fast in me, and thy hand presseth me sore."** David recognized that the first effect of sin on man was that God would rebuke and chasten him. Just as a parent would a disobedient child God has several levels of discipline. He begins by rebuke, or verbal correction. God has given us His word as a verbal reprimand for sin. God has also given preachers to preach against sin and proclaim the hams of it. Just as a child though most do not head the rebuke of God for sin. They persist in sin until God because of His goodness and mercy must take further action. At my home we have a fence. I allow my four small children to play in this fence, enjoying themselves and doing pretty much anything they want to do inside of it. That fence is for their protection, it protects them from the dangers that they are unaware of. It seals them off from speeding cars, strangers, and stray animals. It also keeps them from wandering too far away into other troubles. However, like most children my kids do not see the fence as a good thing. They view the fence as an obstruction to their pleasure. They are convinced that if the fence wasn't there they would be able to have more fun. That may be true for a short period of time but soon they would find the pain of not having the protection I have given them. God has also given us a place of protection, or a fence if you will. His law was given to us for our good. Now no one is justified by the law, and keeping the law will not take any one to heaven. However, when we break the law and get outside of it's boundaries we soon find out that we were better off in the fence. Because just like David we soon find that God Chastens us when we sin. God is not unjust in allowing the chastening effects of sin to come in your life. Quite the opposite, if God did not allow the effects of sin to be hurtful then someday we would stand before him in judgment and say that he was not fair to send us to Hell for our sin since nothing else had ever indicated that there was punishment for our sins.

What Sin Does to Us Emotionally and Physically

David begins to explain the chastening of God in verse three of this chapter when he says, **"There is no soundness in my flesh because of thine anger; neither *is there any* rest in my bones because of my sin."** David says that sin caused guilt and restlessness in him. America is a nation over run with guilt and restlessness. Our society has tried everything know to science to overcome the effects of guilt. What booze and illegal drugs don't cover the pharmacies and doctors are bound and determined to get. Television touts one drug after another to "cure" guilt, worry, anxiety, depression, and every other symptom of sin. These things are not a cure but a worldly band aid, designed to mask the feeling that sin has produced. They only serve to allow mankind to heap to themselves more and more sin for which they will receive judgment. Romans 2:5 tells us, **"But after thy hardness and impenitent heart treasurest up unto thyself wrath against the day of wrath and revelation of the righteous judgment of God;"** The Freudian philosophy that no one is to blame for their own problems, that somehow it is your mothers fault, is a lie. The problem that we have is that our heart is condemning us because of our sin and we are trying to get rid of the guilt by taking drugs and blaming everyone else, instead of taking responsibility for our own sin.

Sin causes many to be restless, and instead of dealing with the sin they try changing everything but their heart. They run from this job to that job, this city to that city, this spouse to that spouse, this church to that church. All the while thinking that some day they will change the right thing so that they will have peace. They never seem to come to the understanding that there is no peace with sin. My mother once told me *"no matter where you go, there you are."* As a young man I thought well of course, what kind of a silly statement is that. I soon learned the truth of what she was saying. If you have problems where you are, you will have problems when you go somewhere else. The problems are not with your environment contrary to what the well known psychologist Skinner said. The problem is with your sinful heart. I heard a preacher wisely say once, *"the heart of every problem is the problem of the heart."* you will not solve your restlessness until you stop trying to change everything and everyone around you and start taking responsibility to change your heart and acknowledge your sin for what it is.

Psalms 38:4 says, **"For mine iniquities are gone over mine head: as an heavy burden they are too heavy for me."** In verse four David continues and tells us that sin brings discouragement and a loss of hope. Suicide is at an epidemic rate in our society. Men and women taking their lives believing that there is no hope, that life is nothing but sorrow and trouble. They take their life hoping to escape the judgment of sin, not realizing that they are headed strait for the eternal judgment. Satan has lied to them and deceived them into believing that nothing could solve the despair of their heart, or ease their burning conscience that is overwhelmed by sin.

Psalms 38:5 goes on to tell us, **"My wounds stink *and* are corrupt because of my foolishness."** Sin brings pain and sickness to man. Doctors have said that 80% of all illness is caused by stress. We have already seen how sin causes stress in life. As you begin to stress over sin, the organs in your body begin to tense up and they stop producing the proper chemicals that you need to be healthy. You stop receiving the necessary amounts of natural chemicals and you will become sick. When you go to the doctor he will give you drugs to compensate for the lack of chemicals but he will not solve the source of the problem. Sickness is an over applied term in our day. We have mental sickness which is a misnomer since the mind is not organic, mental illness is not the same as a brain disease. Mental illness is nothing more many times than man trying to cope with the effects of sin. However, the problems are real. The trauma and complications of life that are caused by sickness and pain because of sin is very real and very hard.

Psalms 38:6 says, **"I am troubled; I am bowed down greatly; I go mourning all the day long."** David entered a deep depression as a result of his sin. Depression is not only caused by sin, but sin can cause depression. When the consequences of our sins are revealed, our response should be repentance, but instead many times we turn to depression, sorrowing over the consequences instead of confessing and repenting of our wickedness. The trouble and grief that comes as a result of sin ought to drive us away from it, but time and again we run headlong into sin thinking that this time it won't hurt me, I won't get caught in the consequences this time. The scriptures say that our sin will find us out, and we will not escape the trouble and grief that it brings.

Psalm 38:7 tells us, **"For my loins are filled with a loathsome *disease*: and *there is* no soundness in my flesh."** Sin not only brings sickness, it brings diseases. Sexually transmitted diseases are epidemic in our world. Africa is overrun with AIDS, and lest you think that we have escaped America is the center for disease control said that in 2006 over 900,000 people had HIV/ AIDS, and that there were 40 - 50 thousand new cases each year in America. This doesn't count the epidemic nature of other sexually transmitted diseases, parents are now putting their Teenage daughters on a pill to make them "one less" to get cervical cancer which is a sexually transmitted disease instead of just teaching them to abstain from sex outside of marriage. When will we wake up and realize that these diseases are a result of sinful lifestyles that are destroying the lives they pretend to enhance. Satan has deceived us into believing that all we need is to stop the consequences and it will be alright, but new consequences just keep popping up. The pill brought the sexual revolution, now you could have sex without consequences, except for the diseases and trail of destroyed lives and homes.

In Psalms 38:8 David declares, **"I am feeble and sore broken: I have roared by reason of the disquietness of my heart."** Sin brings weakness and sorrow, we see so clearly the devastation that sin has brought to David in this passage, yet we still persist on trying it ourselves only to have our strength taken and our hearts destroyed.

In Psalms 38:9-11 David goes on to say, **"Lord, all my desire *is* before thee; and my groaning is not hid from thee. My heart panteth, my strength faileth me: as for the light of mine eyes, it also is gone from me. My lovers and my friends stand aloof from my sore; and my kinsmen stand afar off."** Sin brings a loss of desire, focus, and the senses. It also produces a separation of those who you were closest to. It is amazing how fast our friends and family separate themselves from us when sin is revealed, those that don't are rare indeed. Those you thought were your friends are quickly carried away when the consequences of sin are revealed. The hard truth is that sin will leave you broken, destroyed and alone. It is no wander that God warned us in James 1:15 it says, **"Then when lust hath conceived, it bringeth forth sin: and sin, when it is finished, bringeth forth death."** The word death means separation, when we die physically we are separated from the living. If you are dead spiritually you are separated from God. Sin causes relationships to die as well, and brings a separation between even those we thought loved us.

Psalms 38:12 tells us, **"They also that seek after my life lay snares *for me*: and they that seek my hurt speak mischievous things, and imagine**

deceits all the day long." If it wasn't bad enough that your friends and family forsake you because of sin, it gets worse to think about how your enemies respond when your sin is revealed. They will show no mercy to you. Your misery is their delight. They will make sure that there isn't anyone that doesn't know of your fall and destruction.

As if that was not enough David says in Psalms 38:13-14, **"But I, as a deaf *man*, heard not; and *I was* as a dumb man *that* openeth not his mouth. Thus I was as a man that heareth not, and in whose mouth *are* no reproofs."** Sin leaves you with no answer. I have said many times that sin makes you stupid. It causes you to do things that you would otherwise never do. How many people have made the statement, *"I would never do that,"* only to be the ones falling into the trap laid out. Sin stops the mouth of the transgressor. Romans 3:19 **"Now we know that what things soever the law saith, it saith to them who are under the law: that every mouth may be stopped, and all the world may become guilty before God."** When our hearts are confronted with the law of God, it takes away all our excuses and leaves us without an answer. A man who is still trying to explain away his sin, is still in for trouble. God resists the proud and only gives grace to the humble.

The answer to all of this is found in the last few

verses of this chapter. Psalms 38:15-17 says, **"For in thee, O LORD, do I hope: thou wilt hear, O Lord my God. For I said, *Hear me*, lest *otherwise* they should rejoice over me: when my foot slippeth, they magnify *themselves* against me. For I *am* ready to halt, and my sorrow *is* continually before me."** Notice the first thing David does here is cry out to God. Sin cannot be solved with better prescriptions from your psychiatrist. The consequences of sin must be dealt with by going to God. The next thing we notice is that David made a decision to stop his sin. This is the repentance of his heart. Repentance says, I will not continue doing the things I have been doing. I am ready to stop and I will stop. It is amazing how far many people must go down before they hit the bottom. For some life must become extremely vial before thy will say it is enough. Others persist right into death. Repentance is the first step to overcoming the sin that has devastated life.

Psalms 38:18 tells us, **"For I will declare mine iniquity; I will be sorry for my sin."** The next thing we see is that David confesses his sin. Repentance is first an inward decision, then it produces outward results. Confession is the first step of true repentance, but it is not the last. David declares here that he is sorry for his sin. Notice it doesn't say he is sorry he got caught, or sorry for the cost, no he is sorry for the sin itself. 2 Corinthians 7:10 **"For god-ly sorrow worketh repentance to salvation not to be repented of: but the sorrow of the world worketh death."** The shame we face is that most people are only sorry they got caught. Given the chance they would do it all again, and hope to escape getting caught again. David reveals that there had been a true change in his heart. He was sorry that he had committed sin, not just that he got caught.

The last few verses here teach us what God's response is when we come to Him in true repentance and confession. Psalms 38:19-21 says, **"But mine enemies *are* lively, *and* they are strong: and they that hate me wrongfully are multiplied. They also that render evil for good are mine adversaries; because I follow *the thing that* good *is*. Forsake me not, O LORD: O my God, be not far from me."** We can rejoice because when we come to Him, He does not forsake us. He is not far from the repentant. Psalm 34:18 tells us **"The LORD *is* nigh unto them that are of a broken heart; and saveth such as be of a contrite spirit."** Psalm 51:17 says, **"The sacrifices of God *are* a broken spirit: a broken and a contrite heart, O God, thou wilt not despise."** And Isaiah 57:15 says, **"For thus saith the high and lofty One that inhabiteth eternity, whose name *is* Holy; I dwell in the high and holy *place*, with him also *that is* of a contrite and hum-**

ble spirit, to revive the spirit of the humble, and to revive the heart of the contrite ones."

As David ends he says in Psalms 38:22, "**Make haste to help me, O Lord my salvation.**" Finally we find that God makes haste to help us when we call on Him out of a heart of repentance. What a great truth this is. Just as the father of the prodigal ran to meet him when he returned home, our Heaven Father makes haste to help us when we come to Him in repentance for our sin. Let me conclude this chapter with this, I once heard a message that declared, *"it is as far back as when you left."* That is true, it is as far back to full restoration in the house, but it is never as far back to the forgiveness of the Father. What you will find is what David deals with in the next two chapters, that even after forgiveness the fellowship that you once had doesn't seem the same right away. In the next chapter David seems perplexed because He has not had the restoration that he hoped would come, but then in Chapter 40 he finally reaches that place he longed for. There is a time delay in that process. As you read the next two chapters this process will become clear, but the restoration process cannot start until you come to the end of yourself and return to the Father in repentance.

CHAPTER ELEVEN

The Wilderness

The time between confession and full restoration of joy

Psalm 39:1-13 "I said, I will take heed to my ways, that I sin not with my tongue: I will keep my mouth with a bridle, while the wicked is before me. I was dumb with silence, I held my peace, *even* from good; and my sorrow was stirred. My heart was hot within me, while I was musing the fire burned: *then* spake I with my tongue, LORD, make me to know mine end, and the measure of my days, what it *is*; *that* I may know how frail I *am*. Behold, thou hast made my days *as* an handbreadth; and mine age *is* as nothing before thee: verily every man at his best state *is* altogether vanity. Selah. Surely every man walketh in a vain shew: surely they are disquieted in vain: he heapeth up *riches*, and knoweth not who shall gather them. And now, Lord, what wait I for? my hope *is* in thee. Deliver me from all my transgressions: make me not the reproach of the foolish. I was dumb, I opened not my mouth;

because thou didst *it*. Remove thy stroke away from me: I am consumed by the blow of thine hand. When thou with rebukes dost correct man for iniquity, thou makest his beauty to consume away like a moth: surely every man *is* vanity. Selah. Hear my prayer, O LORD, and give ear unto my cry; hold not thy peace at my tears: for I *am* a stranger with thee, *and* a sojourner, as all my fathers *were*. O spare me, that I may recover strength, before I go hence, and be no more."

Have you ever felt that you are in a spiritual wilderness? There have been several times in my life that I have come to a place such as that. I recall feeling that I could not find the throne of God if I had a road map. I would pray and cry out to God asking why He would not hear me, why he was ignoring me. All the while He did hear me and He was listening to my cry. He was waiting though until I was moldable by Him before He began to speak to me again. Those wilderness times are vital to God's plan for restoring you after you have come to Him in confession of sin.

Psalm 38, 39, and 40 form a trilogy of Psalms that take a journey through the depths of the sorrow of sin in the life of the believer. They begin with Psalm 38 showing us the consequences of sin. Psalm 39 furthers that thought in two areas: first, the emotional state of David after he has confessed his sin, and secondly the residual effects of the physical punishment that God brought on his life as a result of his sin.

Frequently there is a lag time between the confession of our sin, and the restoration of our spirit. There are residual consequences of sin. It would be wonderful if, when we confessed sin and repented, that the consequences just vanished, but they do not, which is why Paul tells us in Galatians 6:9, **"And let us not be weary in well doing: for in due season we shall reap, if we faint not."** The great lesson that we see in the scriptures is that though weeping endures for the night, joy does come in the morning.

As you look at the first several verses of Psalm 40, you see that darkness finally passes as David waits on the Lord. What we are going to examine is the delay time, the time between my repentance and the restoration of the joy of salvation; that is the setting of Psalm 39.

In the H.O.P.E. program I find that this is one of the greatest struggles for people who are saved already and have fallen into sin: that the restoration of joy is not immediate. Because there is a time lag, discouragement can set in and cause someone to turn back to the sinfulness that they have just come out of.

God allows that time lag to be there to try our

sincerity and willingness to depend upon Him rather than ourselves. That time is an estimate of our repentance, whether it was true, or just to get us out of trouble. True repentance knows that what we deserve is Hell, and to serve God without joy in this life is still better than getting what I truly deserve for my sin.

Consider the return of the prodigal in Luke 15. The spirit that he returned with is evident as he says in verse 17-19 of that chapter, **"And when he came to himself, he said, How many hired servants of my father's have bread enough and to spare, and I perish with hunger! I will arise and go to my father, and will say unto him, Father, I have sinned against heaven, and before thee, And am no more worthy to be called thy son: make me as one of thy hired servants."**

Too many people come back to God with the thought that they should be accepted back with full honors and great fanfare. That is not true repentance; there is still pride in their heart. True repentance realizes that I deserve nothing. I don't even deserve to be a servant, it would be the grace of God to make me that much. Should God grant more than that to me would be completely by His abundant grace, but I don't deserve it.

This is exactly what David found in this Psalm. Notice first of all that He recognized He was unworthy of blessings and resigned himself to hold his tongue in the first three verses. **"I said, I will take heed to my ways, that I sin not with my tongue: I will keep my mouth with a bridle, while the wicked is before me. I was dumb with silence, I held my peace, *even* from good; and my sorrow was stirred. My heart was hot within me, while I was musing the fire burned: *then* spake I with my tongue,"**

David felt that he could do nothing right during this time and decided to hold his tongue completely and not say anything. He held his tongue from evil, but he also held it from good. This is the sad state that we come to after sin has damaged us; we become completely uncertain of our walk with God. We don't know which way is up, we can't figure out what is good and what is bad because our judgment has been perverted by sin. David would never have withheld his tongue from good before -- the praises and proclamations of God were continually in his mouth -- yet now in this state he was so out of sorts that he didn't know what to say.

These times of uncertainty and confusion are a direct result of sin aftertaste. 1 Corinthians 14:33 tells us, **"For God is not *the author* of confusion, but of peace, as in all churches of the saints."** This confusion that we go through is not of God, who gives peace, not confusion. Sin however, always brings confusion to the soul.

When David finally does speak he has a grand pity party. He sulks and starts to look at his life and question the purpose of life. Look at verses 4-7, **"LORD, make me to know mine end, and the measure of my days, what it *is*; *that* I may know how frail I *am*. Behold, thou hast made my days as an handbreadth; and mine age *is* as nothing before thee: verily every man at his best state *is* altogether vanity. Selah. Surely every man walketh in a vain shew: surely they are disquieted in vain: he heapeth up *riches*, and knoweth not who shall gather them. And now, Lord, what wait I for? my hope *is* in thee."**

This passage reminds me so much of the book of Ecclesiastes that Solomon David's son would later write after his return to God in his old age. He said in Ecclesiastes 1:2, **"Vanity of vanities, saith the Preacher, vanity of vanities; all *is* vanity."** The word vanity means emptiness, Solomon said that life is nothing but emptiness and nothingness.

That is true if it is lived in sin, and that is exactly where a person comes when they have given their lives to sin. It doesn't matter if that person is lost or saved, they will lose purpose for life when they give into sin.

No doubt David's reprieve here was likely on Solomon's mind as he began to write Ecclesiastes.

David begins to look at his life and say everything he has done is vain. It is empty at its very best.

The truth is that David had accomplished many things for the glory of God. Yet in this state all those things seemed lost to him. The victory that God had given over Goliath, the battles that had been won over the Philistines and all the other enemies of God's people, his anointing to be king by Samuel, and His providential protection by God through the trials of his life were all lost to his mind at this time. He could only see what was immediately before him now.

How true it is that a lifetime of good works can be wiped out by a moment of sin.

As David moves on in verse 8-11 he acknowledges the depth of the effects of God's judgment in his life because of sin. **"Deliver me from all my transgressions: make me not the reproach of the foolish. I was dumb, I opened not my mouth; because thou didst *it*. Remove thy stroke away from me: I am consumed by the blow of thine hand. When thou with rebukes dost correct man for iniquity, thou makest his beauty to consume away like a moth: surely every man *is* vanity. Selah."**

In verse 9 we see that he kept silent because he knew he was under the judgment of God, that it was God that allowed the judgment in his life. Just as a person who experiences a traumatic event in life must come to the place that they acknowledge the hand of God in their lives, so to a person who feels lost and abandoned must acknowledge that God is still in control. He is the one that judges us; He is the one that is right and in control.

When we acknowledge God's hand in our life's trials it takes the power away from our enemy to persecute us any longer. Because God is in control, Satan has no power over us. My earthly enemies have no power over me, if God is in control.

In verses 10 and 11, David speaks of man's inability to stand before the judgment of God. Jesus explained this in Luke 20:18 when He said, **"Whosoever shall fall upon that stone shall be broken; but on whomsoever it shall fall, it will grind him to powder."** You see, if you cast yourself on Jesus in repentance you will be broken as we shall see from David. But if you continue to rebel against Him, persist in sin and refusing to humble yourself to God when His judgment comes upon you it will not just break you, it will destroy you. You will be ground to powder as it were.

David reveals in verse 11 that the judgment of God removes the façade of sin. It is easy to put on the religious face for man. It is easy to pretend to have repented before God. You may convince many that you have changed, but God knows what is in your heart. And when He gets a hold of you, your beautiful façade will be destroyed. Your beauty will consume away like a moth as David puts it. God can quickly reveal the ugly, underlying sin in our lives. Numbers 32:23 says, **"But if ye will not do so, behold, ye have sinned against the LORD: and be sure your sin will find you out."**

The last two verses reveal the state that we must come to if we are going to be restored. It says in verses 12-13, **"Hear my prayer, O LORD, and give ear unto my cry; hold not thy peace at my tears: for I *am* a stranger with thee, *and* a sojourner, as all my fathers *were*. O spare me, that I may recover strength, before I go hence, and be no more."**

David casts himself here on the mercy of God in humility. We must come to a state of complete brokenness before God can truly fix us. We may think that we were already broken, but God has to break the pride before he can remake us into His image as He desires. Until we are totally broken, we are not usable to God.

Jeremiah uses an illustration to show us this principle in Jeremiah 18:1-6 where it says, **"The word which came to Jeremiah from the LORD, saying, Arise, and go down to the potter's house, and there I will cause thee to hear my words. Then I went down to the potter's house, and, behold, he wrought a work on the wheels. And the vessel that he made of clay was marred in the**

hand of the potter: so he made it again another vessel, as seemed good to the potter to make *it*. Then the word of the LORD came to me, saying, O house of Israel, cannot I do with you as this potter? saith the LORD. Behold, as the clay *is* in the potter's hand, so *are* ye in mine hand, O house of Israel."

The potter here is an illustration of the Lord, and we can see how He desires to make us into a vessel of honor so that we will be fit for His use. When we are marred because of sin, He must start over again. It is wonderful to remember that He doesn't throw the clay away; He graciously starts over making us again.

As a young man in high school I took art class and as part of that we had a semester of clay work. We had potters wheels which we had to use, as well as making other types of pots and works. As I began to work with that clay, some things became obvious to me. First, the right amount of water had to be applied to make the clay pliable for use. If the clay was too dry it would break easily. The Scriptures are called the "water of the Word" in Ephesians 5:26. If we have not had a sufficient amount of the Word of God applied in our lives when God seeks to mold us, we can break and become offended. That is why it is vital that a believer be consistent in their devotional life with God.

The second thing that I found was that the clay

had to be completely free from clumps. As the clay was on the wheel, if there was a clump in the clay it would cause it to be marred and break. If the vessel was marred, the bad piece could be pulled out and cast away so that the clay could be pushed down again and I could restart the process of making a vessel. That process always started with adding more water.

Sin in our lives is like the clumps that mar us. As God is trying to produce a vessel of honor out of us, sin must be removed. Then He can begin to re-fashion us according to His will. It is always according to His will that He fashions our lives and not our own will. He is the potter, He is the maker; we are only the material He uses to accomplish His work.

You see, God has a desire to fashion your life into a great vessel of honor that is fit for the master's use, but you must submit to the breaking down of your life for Him to accomplish this. You must admit that you don't know what is best for yourself, as Jeremiah said in Jeremiah 10:23, **"O LORD, I know that the way of man *is* not in himself: *it is* not in man that walketh to direct his steps."**

You have to come to Him as the prodigal did without expectations and in true repentance, understanding that He is not obligated to restore you, it is only by His grace that He does so.

CHAPTER TWELVE

Biblical Restoration

Psalm 40:1-17 "I waited patiently for the LORD; and he inclined unto me, and heard my cry. He brought me up also out of an horrible pit, out of the miry clay, and set my feet upon a rock, *and* established my goings. And he hath put a new song in my mouth, even praise unto our God: many shall see *it*, and fear, and shall trust in the LORD. Blessed *is* that man that maketh the LORD his trust, and respecteth not the proud, nor such as turn aside to lies. Many, O LORD my God, *are* thy wonderful works *which* thou hast done, and thy thoughts *which are* to us-ward: they cannot be reckoned up in order unto thee: *if* I would declare and speak *of them*, they are more than can be numbered. Sacrifice and offering thou didst not desire; mine ears hast thou opened: burnt offering and sin offering hast thou not required. Then said I, Lo, I come: in the volume of the book *it is* written of me, I delight to do thy will, O my God: yea,

thy law *is* within my heart. I have preached righteousness in the great congregation: lo, I have
not refrained my lips, O LORD, thou know-
est. I have not hid thy righteousness within my
heart; I have declared thy faithfulness and thy
salvation: I have not concealed thy lovingkindness and thy truth from the great congregation.
Withhold not thou thy tender mercies from me,
O LORD: let thy lovingkindness and thy truth
continually preserve me. For innumerable evils
have compassed me about: mine iniquities have
taken hold upon me, so that I am not able to look
up; they are more than the hairs of mine head:
therefore my heart faileth me. Be pleased, O
LORD, to deliver me: O LORD, make haste to
help me. Let them be ashamed and confounded
together that seek after my soul to destroy it; let
them be driven backward and put to shame that
wish me evil. Let them be desolate for a reward
of their shame that say unto me, Aha, aha. Let all
those that seek thee rejoice and be glad in thee:
let such as love thy salvation say continually, The
LORD be magnified. But I *am* poor and needy;
yet the Lord thinketh upon me: thou *art* my help
and my deliverer; make no tarrying, O my God."

Psalm 40 is a Psalm of restoration and joy. It
shows us the blessing of renewed fellowship and
what awaits us if we will patiently wait on the Lord.

No matter how you feel, the Lord will not withhold His joy from you forever; He will hear your cry and answer you in His time.

Verses one through five here speak about the joy of restoration. David has been through the repentant return, and the wilderness of waiting, but now He says that the Lord has heard him, and he has a new standing. It is wonderful to know that you are on a rock.

In Palm 61:2 David says, **"From the end of the earth will I cry unto thee, when my heart is overwhelmed: lead me to the rock *that* is higher than I."** It is good to remember and reflect on the pit that God has taken you from. If we are not careful, we forget the wickedness that we were in and just how far God has taken us from it. We get proud in our own flesh and begin to depend upon our strength at those times.

Remember the pit from which we were dug keeps us humble and dependent upon God.

Not only did David have a new standing, but he also had a new song. In Psalm 39 he had no song but that of sorrow. He was seeking death, but now after patiently waiting for the Lord he has a song of praise to our God.

If we could only remember this truth, that praise is the pathway to joy. We tend to sit and wallow in the Mulley-grubs and poor-me's as if staying there would help us to feel better, but it never does. God tells us in Isaiah 61:3 **"To appoint unto them that mourn in Zion, to give unto them beauty for ashes, the oil of joy for mourning, the garment of praise for the spirit of heaviness; that they might be called trees of righteousness, the planting of the LORD, that he might be glorified."**

The purpose of this song was not just for David, though he was surely a benefactor of it as it lifted his spirit. The great power of his song was that others would hear and trust in the Lord. Often because we refuse to praise the Lord in the wilderness periods of our life, we offer up a poor testimony of our God to this world.

Anyone can praise Him when everything is going well, but to praise Him after bad things is a testimony to the sustaining power of our God.

The next thing we see in David is a renewed hope. He is blessed and happy because he has put his trust back where it belongs -- in the Lord. Jeremiah 17:5 says, **"Thus saith the LORD; Cursed *be* the man that trusteth in man, and maketh flesh his arm, and whose heart departeth from the LORD."** What a contrast to what David is experiencing here; he is blessed not cursed. This doesn't mean that everything in your life is always going perfectly, but it does mean that you accept God's perfect will for your life.

In Psalm 39 David knew that God was in control of everything, but in Psalm 40 He is rejoicing in that truth. He begins to recount God's control through His many wonderful works. It is good to do that often. How long has it been since you just sat down and rehearsed back to God all the things that He has done for you? It will change your outlook on life I assure you.

Not only are God's works great toward us, but also His thoughts are great toward us. Sometimes a person will come up to me and say they were thinking about me or praying for me. That means so much to me, but to consider that God's thoughts are so great toward me that they cannot be numbered just blows me away.

God, who controls everything in the universe, who sustains all of life, who sees everything and yet His thoughts toward you are more than can be numbered. What an awesome thing!

When you are in the wilderness time you don't think that God is thinking about you at all, yet when your joy is restored by Him, you find that His thoughts about you are so many that there isn't a number big enough to express them.

When I first met my wife, we fell madly in love. I thought about her all the time. I wanted to speak to her all the time just to hear what she had to say. I wanted to write to her just so she would respond back to me with another love letter. It was like that when I got saved as well. I wanted to fellowship with God completely, I wanted to be in His Word all the time because it was fresh and new.

Yet, somehow the older I became in the Lord, the more I found that there were times that I didn't consider Him at all in my thoughts. The same is true in my marriage. Sometimes I can become so selfish in my relationship with my wife and my thoughts are not toward her. However, not once did God's thoughts of me ever diminish. Not once did He forget about me. When my heart is right, I repent of the wicked selfishness that I have been in and seek to restore that wonderful fellowship I once had.

So how is it that God's joy was restored to David? It was by a process we call imputation. Imputation means that it was nothing that David did; it was all of God.

Sometimes when in the wilderness, we begin to bargain with God: God if you will restore my joy, I will make sacrifices in my life. God doesn't want you to make sacrifices; He wants you to reject your own works and remember that fellowship with Him isn't now and never has been about what you do; it is always about what He did. Fellowship with God doesn't have to be work; it is just resting in Him. Throughout the Bible, God pleads with us to reject our own works and to cast ourselves on Him and trust Him.

Your plan of drawing close to God won't work anyway because your plan is just a dead religion. It is no different than any other dead religion -- it is about you. God has to draw you close; you cannot do it alone.

He has already atoned for your sins and your joy is not dependent upon another sacrifice. You joy is dependent upon what David speaks of in verse seven when He says, **"Then said I, Lo, I come: in the volume of the book it *is* written of me,"** This verse is messianic; it is speaking of Jesus. It is quoted again in Hebrews 10:7 showing that it was speaking of Jesus.

God didn't desire a sacrifice from David, and He doesn't desire one from you. He desired the sacrifice of Jesus Christ. The imputation of joy comes as a result of the rejection of my own works, plans, and schemes and my acceptance of the finished work of Jesus Christ. I can add nothing to His work to make me more acceptable to God. He did it all.

We continue to go back to the old way of thinking though, believing that if I made some sacrifice God would accept me again, elevating our works and deeds to be equal with those of the Lord. We forget that if we are saved, we are already accepted in the beloved; we already have victory through the finished work of Christ. This is a truth and reality, and my sacrifice is nothing, He made the only sacrifice acceptable to God. The joy of the Lord is not dependent on what I do, but rather on yielding myself to what He has done.

The key to the Christian life is yielding to the Spirit of God. The joy is in the acceptance that Jesus has paid your penalty and you are a child of God, forgiven and purged, accepted in Him by God. Your job now is not to find another sacrifice, but to live in His Spirit.

We must glory in the finished work of Jesus, rather than labor to earn God's acceptance. Jesus told us in Matthew 11 to take His yoke upon us because it is easy, and His burden is light. Trying to live the Christian life in your own power is neither easy nor light. It is hard; no it is impossible to live the Christian life by your own power.

God says in Zechariah 4:6 "**Then he answered and spake unto me, saying, This *is* the word of the LORD unto Zerubbabel, saying, Not by might, nor by power, but by my spirit, saith the LORD of hosts.**" It is only possible to live the Christian life by His Spirit. That is why you stay in the wilderness so long, because you are still trying to get back to fellowship with God by your works, rather than casting them off and depending totally on Him.

Once you realize the joy of imputation, you must also consider the joy of preservation. Remember that the evil that once overcame you is still present; only in Jesus is there safety from sin. It is when you wander away from His presence that you can be overcome again.

A passage in Proverbs has been a great help to me over the years. It says in Proverbs 30:24-28 **"There be four *things which are* little upon the earth, but they *are* exceeding wise: The ants *are* a people not strong, yet they prepare their meat in the summer; The conies *are but* a feeble folk, yet make they their houses in the rocks; The locusts have no king, yet go they forth all of them by bands; The spider taketh hold with her hands, and is in kings' palaces."**

I often consider these four groups, because they have a great lesson for me. When I begin to think that I am big and can handle sin, that is when I get crushed by sin. But, if I will be wise as these are wise, I can dwell in the King's palace. My favorite of these are the conies. I jokingly told my kids that these were small brown tube-like creatures that were about 6 inches long with no eyes or legs, and that is where we get hot dogs. They didn't believe me though.

In the margin of one of my study Bibles it said that these were badgers, but if you have ever had a dealing with a badger, you would disagree. Badgers are not feeble. As a young man I helped my dad with our farm by plowing the fields with the tractor. One day I ran over a badger den and out came that badger and attacked the tractor. Of course he was no match for the tractor, but the next time I came around he came after me again.

As I said, badgers are not feeble folk, and they do not make their abode in the rocks. The conies are small rabbit-like creatures. They are frail and feeble, and they know that they are no match for the predators. So they live where they cannot be destroyed.

You and I would be wise to remember how feeble we are, and keep ourselves in the Rock of Jesus Christ. In Him is where our safety and security is, God's protection never left you, you left it. As long as you and I maintain our relationship with Christ, there is protection.

What a great refuge God is to His children; we should glory in the refuge of His grace. Notice what David says in verse 16 of Psalm 40, **"Let all those that seek thee rejoice and be glad in thee: let such as love thy salvation say continually, The LORD be magnified."** The LORD be magnified indeed!

Who loves the salvation of the Lord? Those who abide in His presence and those who recognize that they were in a pit and He pulled them out. Those who have a new song in their mouth and have chosen to be in the fellowship of God, abiding in the Rock of their salvation will have joy. That is where the joy is, it is in rejection of our own works, and closeness to Him.

Wait patiently upon the Lord and cast off your own sacrifices and works, and He will restore your joy.